FIRST NATIONS WILDFIRE EVACUATIONS

A GUIDE FOR COMMUNITIES AND EXTERNAL AGENCIES

TARA K. MCGEE and
AMY CARDINAL CHRISTIANSON
with the **First Nations Wildfire
Evacuation Partnership**

PURICH
BOOKS

T0350641

30 29 28 27 26 25 24 23 22   5 4 3 2

Printed in Canada on FSC-certified ancient-forest-free paper
(100% post-consumer recycled) that is processed chlorine- and acid-free.

Library and Archives Canada Cataloguing in Publication

Title: First Nations wildfire evacuations : a guide for communities and external
     agencies / Tara K. McGee and Amy Cardinal Christianson ; with the First Nations
     Wildfire Evacuation Partnership.
Names: McGee, Tara K., author. | Cardinal Christianson, Amy, author. | First Nations
     Wildfire Evacuation Partnership, author.
Description: Includes bibliographical references and index.
Identifiers: Canadiana (print) 20200398652 | Canadiana (ebook) 20200398725 |
     ISBN 9780774880664 (softcover) | ISBN 9780774880671 (PDF) |
     ISBN 9780774880688 (EPUB)
Subjects: LCSH: Evacuation of civilians – Canada. | LCSH: Emergency management –
     Canada – Handbooks, manuals, etc. | LCSH: Emergency management – Canada –
     Planning. | LCSH: Wildfires – Canada – Safety measures. | LCSH: Indigenous
     peoples – Canada.
Classification: LCC HV554 .M34 2021 | DDC 363.37/808997071—dc23

Canadä

UBC Press gratefully acknowledges the financial support for our publishing program of
the Government of Canada (through the Canada Book Fund) and the British Columbia
Arts Council.

Printed and bound in Canada by Friesens
Set in Noto Serif and Fira Sans by Gerilee McBride
Substantive and copy editor: Lesley Erickson
Proofreader: Helen Godolphin
Indexer: Patricia Buchanan
Cartographer: Eric Leinberger
Cover designer: Gerilee McBride
Cover images: *front (top) and back,* detail from *Sunfire,* by Karen Erickson; *front (bottom),*
     barricade during the 2011 evacuation of Whitefish Lake, by Jimmy Grey

Purich Books, an imprint of UBC Press
2029 West Mall
Vancouver, BC V6T 1Z2
www.purichbooks.ca

CONTENTS

Foreword

AS THE PRESIDENT of the Tahltan Central Government, it is an honour to be given the opportunity to welcome readers to this book on First Nations wildfire evacuations. This is an incredibly important topic and one that our Nation is unfortunately all too familiar with.

The Tahltan Nation is located in northwestern British Columbia, covering a vast territory the size of Portugal, where we and our ancestors have lived for thousands of years. Tahltan people, who boast a population of about 4,000, are easily outnumbered by grizzly bears, mountain goats, wolves, and other iconic Canadian species in our homelands. Prior to the exposure of foreign diseases and colonization, Tahltans lived a nomadic lifestyle in the subarctic climate and environment. Our territory is vast and rich in natural resources and culture, but the remoteness coupled with climate change create geographic vulnerabilities when faced with an environmental crisis.

The local Tahltan communities of Dease Lake, Iskut, and Telegraph Creek have no cell service or other common facilities and stores that most Canadians take for granted. Each community has one gas station, a small school, and a clinic. Telegraph Creek, known as Tlegohin in the local language, has no paved roads and is nearly seven hundred kilometres away from the nearest commercial airport, bank, or fast-food restaurant. It usually has around three hundred and fifty residents, most of whom are Tahltan people living on the federal reserve lands administered by the Tahltan Band Council under the Indian Act.

It was August 3rd, 2018, when I received the call about an emergency quickly developing near Telegraph Creek. A lightning strike from the evening before had created a fire which was picking up momentum from the coastal winds and high temperatures. Due to the lack of properly trained emergency personnel, equipment, and facilities in the community, the local leaders found themselves in a difficult position as an imminent threat suddenly became more serious. As is the case for many of the First Nations communities profiled in this book, word of the fire spread quickly on social media and around the camping grounds that everyone might be forced to evacuate if the situation worsened overnight. To make matters worse, Tahltans from all over BC, the Yukon, and even the United States were arriving in Telegraph Creek to visit relatives and attend the local annual music festival.

Less than two days later, on August 5th, Chief Rick McLean of the Tahltan Band and his team worked alongside the RCMP to evacuate all the local residents – an experience that is familiar to the wildfire evacuees who share their stories in this book. My father, a Tahltan Elder born and raised in the community, was one such evacuee who left his home just a couple of hours after the RCMP went door-to-door posting notices and telling everyone to get prepared to leave town. In the final hours leading up to the mass evacuation, other Tahltans tuned in attentively on Facebook to watch live videos being posted of the bright orange waves of fire spilling over top of the mountainous terrain and heading directly toward Telegraph Creek. Everyone in the community, aside from three stubborn and heroic men, were shuttled out in vehicles toward Dease Lake.

Julien Du, Mickie Ferguson, and Marty Nole were the three men who decided to stay behind to help save what they could. The trio worked as a unit to utilize a handful of sprinkler systems and whatever other resources they could find. If the fire pushed them to the edge of the community, they each had access to a motorized boat stocked with fuel and other goods which could lead them to safety. As the authors of *First Nations Wildfire Evacuations* make clear, often some community members feel the need to remain behind to try and protect their communities, and they should be allowed to do so when they have a plan that enables them to safely escape, because of our inherent right to protect our territory.

The Tahltan Nation Development Corporation (TNDC), well-known for its expertise with earthworks construction, quickly responded and worked with the province to ensure Tahltan crews were in the field contributing. Their crews built fireguards and did everything else they could to save homes, cultural sites, and other important infrastructure. The TNDC team risked their lives and long-term health while enduring smoky conditions for 12+-hour shifts for several weeks. The province also deployed aircraft and additional firefighter support to Telegraph Creek from multiple jurisdictions. Helicopters scooped up water from nearby Sawmill Lake and the Stikine River, while other aircraft dropped fire retardant all over the hillsides surrounding the community.

As several brave teams battled the fires together, most of the displaced evacuees stayed in the neighbouring communities of Dease Lake and Iskut with family members. Others travelled to nearby cities with high concentrations of Tahltan people, such as Smithers, Terrace, and Whitehorse. Some stayed with family and friends while others choose to live in hotels. Extra support systems were put in place for Elders and those with young children. As this book makes clear, having a strategy in place for where to evacuate to, and how to support Elders and young families once evacuated, is an important part of planning for evacuations.

Fundraising efforts and own-source revenues from industrial projects allowed Tahltan governments to provide additional funding to evacuees. From the early stages of the evacuation, public donations of every sort – including food, water, fuel, clothing, and household items – started arriving by the truckload from across BC and the Yukon to distribution centres where evacuees had fled.

Over twenty homes, cultural sites, and many community structures – including a church and the nursing residence – were destroyed in the fires. Additional fires in the area eventually joined together to create further challenges throughout the summer. About 150,000 hectares of Tahltan territory were affected by the fires that year and British Columbia had the worst wildfire season in its history, with over 2,100 fires burning through 1.3 million hectares of land.

Once the BC Wildfire Service downgraded the fire in late August, power and telephone lines, drinking water, and septic facilities all needed extensive assessment and repairs. Crews had to clear dangerous trees and other hazards, while others inspected slope stability and repaired portions of the community's only access road. During a visit to Telegraph Creek in the fall, Canada's Minister of Indigenous Services at the time, Jane Philpott, noted that "the Tahltan Nation itself incurred the worst structural damage caused by wildfires of any First Nations community in recorded Canadian history."

The evacuation order lasted a total of 102 days, as it took a couple of months to sort through the logistics of replacing hydro poles/lines, testing the banks of the Telegraph Creek road for stability/safety, fixing waterlines and so on in the community, and cleaning the remaining homes and properties because of the smoke and ash that found their way inside via ventilation systems or open windows.

Although the losses were considerable and historic, we must acknowledge the incredible and heroic efforts of the crews who saved the essential infrastructure and the vast majority of homes in and around Telegraph Creek. Had it not been for TNDC's capacity and timeliness, along with some very collaborative Tahltan leadership and partnerships, the majority of Telegraph Creek would not be standing today. Most residents were back in their homes or moved into new residences in time for Christmas and the children were attending the local school again shortly thereafter.

Over the past two years, Telegraph Creek's clean-up, recovery, and rebuild expenditures have totalled nearly thirty million dollars. The environmental impacts are apparent with more flooding and landslides along the areas with displaced forests and root systems; several wildlife populations and species have relocated too. Many areas formerly known for their immense beauty and greenery, such as the forests along the Stikine Canyon, remain blackened and unrecognizable due to the fires.

As this book shows, Indigenous peoples across Canada – and around the world – are incredibly adaptable and able to rise to the challenges wildfires may bring to their communities. Like the burned landscapes, the cumulative impacts of the fires has changed the Tahltan Nation and the ways that we will prepare ourselves and deal with future environmental emergencies. We are rebuilding our community and healing from the pain with each passing day. Like our ancestors before us, we remain proud, strong, and resilient people who will continue to thrive in Tahltan territory for generations to come.

Chad Norman Day
President, Tahltan Central Government

Preface

INDIGENOUS NATIONS in Canada have lived since time immemorial with wildfire threats. In recent years, they have been evacuated when threatened by either fire proximity, wildfire smoke, or interruptions to essential services (such as power loss caused by a wildfire burning a power line or electricity substation). People who live in urban settings in Canada may be affected by wildfire smoke when it drifts in. They are told to limit their time outdoors and to avoid participating in extreme physical activities. Few realize that Indigenous Peoples often live on the frontlines of this hazard.

In 2011 alone, 4,216 wildfires burned 2.6 million hectares of forest throughout Canada. First Nations communities were severely affected. Thousands of residents from thirty-five communities were forced to evacuate their lands because of their proximity to wildfire or smoke. Many went to nearby towns; others evacuated to towns and cities a considerable distance away; some stayed in their own or another First Nation. Some left by road, others by air.

This book is the result of research from the First Nations Wildfire Evacuation Partnership, which was formed shortly after the 2011 wildfires. Tara McGee, a non-Indigenous professor at the University of Alberta who studies the human dimensions of wildland fire, was speaking with Larry Fremont of Saskatchewan's Ministry of Environment. Larry mentioned that one of the First Nations in his province had experienced difficulties during its evacuation. Shortly after the phone call, Tara contacted Amy Cardinal Christianson, a Métis research scientist at the Canadian Forest Service whose research focuses on wildfire and Indigenous Peoples. Amy enthusiastically jumped on board, and the First Nations Wildfire Evacuation Partnership was born.

From its inception, two key questions guided the project:

- How have First Nation peoples and communities been affected by wildfire evacuations?
- How can the negative effects of these evacuations be reduced?

Because the 2011 wildfires caused the evacuation of many First Nations in Ontario, Saskatchewan, and Alberta, we focused on these three provinces and identified six First Nations that had been recently evacuated: in Ontario, Mishkeegogamang Ojibway Nation, Sandy Lake First Nation, and Deer Lake First Nation; in Saskatchewan, Onion Lake First Nation; and in Alberta, Whitefish Lake First Nation 459 and Dene Tha' First Nation (Taché community). We then contacted community leaders in these Nations, introduced ourselves and the partnership, and invited the First Nations to become involved in developing and carrying out the research. Community leaders in all six Nations expressed interest and invited us to meet in person with their band councils. During these meetings, we discussed the research, learned about the First Nations, and heard about their evacuations. One year into our research, in 2014, Lac La Ronge Indian Band, Stanley Mission, in Saskatchewan, was evacuated. We invited them to join the partnership, and they agreed, bringing the number of participating communities to seven.

To ensure that our research would make a difference, we also involved government and nongovernmental agencies. Amy recruited the following partners:

Indigenous	Assembly of First Nations (David Diabo and Irving Leblanc) First Nations' Emergency Services Society (Shane Wardrobe)
Alberta	Alberta Emergency Management Agency (Fran Byers) Agriculture and Forestry (Chad Morrison)

Saskatchewan	Ministry of Environment (Larry Fremont)
	Ministry of Government Relations
	(Carl Friske and Deanna Valentine)
	Ministry of Health (Garnet Matchett)
Ontario	Emergency Management Ontario
	(Aadu Pilt and Rebecca Hanson)
	Ministry of Natural Resources and Forestry
	(Rob McAlpine and Bill Cole)
Federal	Indigenous Services Canada (Dianne Carlson,
	Eileen McCarthy, and Michelle Ring)
	Health Canada (Wadieh Yacoub and
	Wojciech Drobina)

Once we secured funding from the Social Sciences and Humanities Research Council's Partnership Development Grant competition, the First Nations Wildfire Evacuation Partnership officially started. Two graduate students, Kyla Mottershead and Henok Asfaw, then joined the research team.

Each band chose community advisers to represent them in the research, and seven community research assistants were hired to help recruit interview participants and conduct interviews (see "A Note on the Partnership" for a full account). We interviewed more than two hundred former evacuees, but we also talked to people who had helped carry out or provide support during the evacuations, and we talked to residents who chose to stay behind despite evacuation orders.

Rather than simply reporting on what we learned from the seven communities, we decided to present this knowledge in the form of a guidebook for First Nations, external agencies, and host communities. As we learned, each First Nation had a different experience: some were good, some were bad. Participants shared their stories openly with us, despite it being hard for many of them. A few told us it was the only opportunity they had to talk about what happened. Others said they wanted to make sure the outside world knew what their experience had been like. There was a strong desire to share their experiences so that future evacuations of other First Nations (or their own) would go better. To make sure this happens, this book documents their experiences and offers a step-by-step guide to developing an evacuation plan and carrying it out – from how to decide to evacuate to what to do when community members finally return home.

Partial profits from the sale of this book will be gifted to the Susan Jensen Indigenous Support Fund, Faculty of Science, University of Alberta, and Yukon First Nations Wildfire, a top-tier wildfire-fighting service.

Community Partners

Deer Lake First Nation, Ontario

This Oji-Cree First Nation, connected by a seasonal ice road to Sandy Lake First Nation in the winter, is a small fly-in community located near the Manitoba border in Ontario's Far North. Residents at high risk from wildfire smoke were evacuated in a partial evacuation via Canadian Forces Hercules aircraft early in July 2011 and then again two weeks later as wildfire again came close to the community.

Dene Tha' (/'dɛnɛ ða:/) First Nation, Taché, Alberta

The Dene Tha' community of Taché is located in the northwestern corner of Alberta on the Mackenzie Highway (Highway 35). Heavy wildfire smoke from the Lutose Complex Fire led to its evacuation in July 2012. Residents had little time to prepare and were unfamiliar with evacuation processes. Despite these and other significant issues, Taché used local resources and personnel to carry out the evacuation with little outside assistance.

Lac La Ronge Indian Band, Stanley Mission (Amuchewaspimewin), Saskatchewan

The Lac La Ronge Indian Band, Stanley Mission, is a Woodland Cree community located in north-central Saskatchewan. Stanley Mission was evacuated due to the Lagoon Fire in May 2014 and then one year later due to the Egg Fire in June 2015. The first evacuation was a partial evacuation for those at high risk from wildfire smoke but escalated to a full evacuation when fire threatened the access road and power lines.

Mishkeegogamang Ojibway Nation, Ontario
This Ojibwe First Nation is located in northwestern Ontario and accessible year-round by Highway 599. In 2011, the Sioux Lookout Fire 35 led to a ten-day evacuation. Mishkeegogamang is divided into two parts. Reserve 63A is on the south shore of Lake St. Joseph, and Reserve 63B is to the north of the lake, surrounding Dog Hole Bay.

Onion Lake (wîhcekaskosîwi-sâkahikanihk) Cree Nation, Saskatchewan
Located on the Alberta-Saskatchewan border fifty kilometres north of Lloydminster, this First Nation has two highways that run through its reserves, which frequently experience wildfire. The community experienced partial evacuations in 2012 and 2013. Onion Lake handled the emergencies internally with little assistance from outside government agencies.

Sandy Lake First Nation (Neh gaaw saga'igan), Ontario
This Oji-Cree First Nation is located seventy kilometres northeast of Deer Lake First Nation in Ontario's Far North. It, like Deer Lake, is a fly-in community; it is connected in the winter to Deer Lake and North Spirit Lake via an ice road. When the ice clears, it also connects to Keewaywin First Nation by boat. In 2011, this large fly-in community was evacuated by Canadian Forces Hercules aircraft.

Whitefish Lake First Nation 459 (Atikameg), Alberta
Located in north-central Alberta about an hour northeast of Slave Lake, this community is accessible by Highway 750 and the Bicentennial Highway (AB-88). The Utikuma Complex Fires caused an evacuation in May 2011. The evacuation lasted two weeks for most evacuees and three weeks for pregnant women, families with babies, and residents with pre-existing health issues.

First Nations Wildfire Evacuations

Introduction

IT BEGINS WITH the smoke.

Someone from the nation will see a smoke plume, either nearby or far away, and almost immediately an image will appear on social media – "Did you see the smoke!?" A quiet unease then ripples through the community. Wildfires in the summer are nothing new for First Nations in the boreal forest, and everyone understands that the risk is real.

It often happens on a hot day, when warm winds gust. The smoke plume expands, and ash spreads through the upper atmosphere, turning the sun a disconcerting orange. In need of reassurance, people call the band office or their families. Band staff search for information and try to determine the position of the fire and whether it's a threat.

When the ash starts to fall, everyone knows that things are getting serious. What was once beautiful – black ash floating like tiny feathers in an orange sky – now collects like ground grey chalk on car hoods, a platform for curious children to write their names. The day begins to darken as the smoke blocks out the sun. Day quickly turns to night, and visibility becomes limited to a few metres, at best. Those who have respiratory conditions such as asthma begin to experience difficulties breathing, and then ash and embers at ground level make it physically difficult for even healthy people to breathe.

The band reaches out to multiple agencies – local, provincial, and federal for advice on whether to evacuate. Although the smoke seems to be near and poses a threat to community members, they have no idea how close the fire is to the community. The actual flame front could be many kilometres away. But rumours continue to circulate. If the First Nation is accessible by road, some people might simply get in their vehicles and leave before an evacuation is called. For those who live in fly-in communities, it's not that easy. In both cases, residents must depend on leaders and outside agencies to ensure their safety. There are often no set protocols or guidelines in place, even though First Nations are some of the most at-risk communities in Canada and it has been predicted that their at-risk status will only increase with climate change.

If you live in a First Nation and are responsible for or concerned about wildfire evacuations, or if you work for an outside agency and need or want to know about the special concerns and needs of First Nations, this book is for you, though it will also be a valuable resource for other Indigenous and non-Indigenous communities in Canada and beyond. Indigenous peoples around the world have lived with fire for tens of thousands of years and have specialized fire knowledge which has been passed down through generations. Unfortunately, as a result of colonization, many Indigenous communities have been unable to practice their fire management techniques to protect their communities from fire.

This is troubling because it is well established that climate change is causing more extreme wildfires around the world, and that many of these fires directly affect Indigenous communities. During the unprecedented Australian wildfires of early 2020, for example, Indigenous peoples in Australia in both New South Wales and Victoria were evacuated. Later the same year, the Slater fire in Northern California burned into the community of Happy Camp in the Klamath National Forest, home to many members of the Karuk Tribe. That fire killed two people and destroyed over a hundred properties.

The Ongoing Problem
with Emergency Preparedness

In the mid-1990s, researchers examined the emergency preparedness of three First Nations in Manitoba. They found that past evacuations from wildfires and flooding had been hampered by communication difficulties, insufficient information, and inadequate evacuation plans, which caused chaos, confusion, and delay, putting further stress on evacuees. There were instances where residents were separated from immediate family members during the evacuation. Almost twenty-five years after the initial research, emergency preparedness continues to be a problem.

In the 2010s, an evacuation from a remote fly-in community in Saskatchewan faced similar challenges, but the problems were compounded by the fact that the wildfire occurred during a band council election. There was no official government to lead the evacuation.

The 2013 fall report of the Auditor General of Canada's office included a chapter devoted to emergency management on reserves, which identified these issues:

1 Responsibility for emergency management on reserves among stakeholders was unclear.
2 Program authorities were out of date, and regional plans and supporting guidelines had not been completed.
3 A risk-based, all-hazards approach to emergency management was not in place.
4 The budget for the emergency-management program was not sufficient, and support focused on response-and-recovery activities.
5 The funding process was complex and contained internal control weaknesses.
6 The monitoring and reporting of performance information was incomplete.
7 Federal departmental roles and responsibilities and risk management for health emergencies could be strengthened.
8 Pandemic plans did not exist in all First Nations communities.
9 There was limited coordination between Aboriginal Affairs and Northern Development Canada (now Indigenous Services Canada) and Health Canada.

Although Indigenous peoples around the world are incredibly diverse and the contexts in which they may need to evacuate can look very different, the experiences of the First Nations in this book offer lessons to anyone who wants to prepare for a possible wildfire evacuation. Government policies and the kind of support that is available to communities may vary from country to country, but the stages of an evacuation are often very similar. This book will help emergency planners think about what they can do to improve communication with community members, how to keep families together during evacuations, how to prioritize care for Elders and other vulnerable community members, and to think about what kind of food and activities would help evacuees feel more comfortable. Importantly, it also addresses the need to celebrate returns to communities after an evacuation.

Drawing on the evacuation experiences of residents from seven First Nations in Ontario, Saskatchewan, and Alberta between 2011 and 2015, along with a few other examples, this book offers a detailed account of what has happened, what can happen, and what should happen during the six stages of an evacuation:

- deciding to evacuate
- putting a plan in motion
- troubleshooting transportation
- finding accommodations
- taking care of evacuees
- returning home.

Each chapter corresponds to one of these stages and includes checklists and guiding questions for First Nations, external agencies, and host communities. Spotlights on each of the seven First Nations appear before and after each of the six chapters.

But before exploring the issues and experiences of particular First Nations, it's important to understand the special circumstances of First Nations in general when it comes to wildfires.

On average, 8,400 wildfires burn over 2 to 4 million hectares of forest every year in Canada. Although Indigenous Peoples make up only 4.9 percent of the population, nearly one-third of wildfire evacuations involve Indigenous Peoples, who in Canada comprise three groups: First Nations, Métis, and Inuit. This book focuses on the evacuation experiences of First Nations people who were evacuated from their communities.

Spotlights on Community Partners

Seven unique First Nations participated in the First Nations Wildfire Evacuation Partnership and lend their voices to this book. To read more about a particular First Nation, check out its spotlight.

Ontario	Mishkeegogamang Ojibway Nation (p. 83)
	Sandy Lake First Nation (p. 103)
	Deer Lake First Nation (p. 67)
Saskatchewan	Onion Lake Cree Nation (p. 121)
	Lac La Ronge Indian Band, Stanley Mission (p. 47)
Alberta	Whitefish Lake First Nation 459 (p. 11)
	Dene Tha' First Nation, Taché (p. 29)

First Nations have lived in the territory now known as Canada since time immemorial. There are currently 634 recognized First Nations spread throughout the country. Although people often talk about First Nations in collective terms, each First Nation is distinct in terms of territory, cultural practices, languages, spirituality, and traditions. European colonization, which began to spread across Canada in the 1600s, continues to this day. Land, children, and culture have been stolen from First Nations through various government programs such as the establishment of reserves (including the pass system), disenfranchisement, residential schools, child "welfare" programs like the Sixties Scoop, and the outlawing of cultural activities. First Nations people fall under the jurisdiction of the federal government in a relationship that has always been paternalistic.

> Between 1980 and 2019, 389 First Nations communities were evacuated in Canada because of wildfire, with approximately 138,000 evacuees.

The majority of First Nations communities are located on reserves that may or may not be their Traditional Territory. There are also many First Nations people who belong to a specific Nation but live off-reserve, generally in more urban settings. The First Nations Wildfire Evacuation Partnership focused on community members who live on reserve who were evacuated. The Canadian Forest Service reports that 60 percent of 3,105 reserves – that is, 1,871 reserves – either lie within or intersect with the wildland-urban interface, where communities are at higher risk from wildfire because of their proximity to boreal forest. Between 1980 and 2019, 389 First Nations communities were evacuated in Canada because of wildfire, with approximately 138,000 evacuees. In 2011 alone, twenty-nine First Nations communities were forced to evacuate, and some communities have had to evacuate multiple times. For example, one of the community partners, Lac La Ronge Indian Band, evacuated one or more of their reserves in Saskatchewan fourteen times between 1980 and 2017. In the same period, the Neskantaga First Nation and Nibinamik First Nation settlement of Summer Beaver, Ontario, were evacuated twelve times. Some First Nations may even be evacuated multiple times in one summer. Another community partner, Deer Lake First Nation, for instance, was evacuated twice in July 2011. Five hundred residents were evacuated in a partial evacuation on July 6. They returned home on July 13, but just over one week later, on July 21, a second partial evacuation occurred.

The Canadian Forest Service predicts that, with climate change, fire-prone conditions will increase by one and a half to four times and that First Nations will see an increased risk of wildfire compared to non-Indigenous communities because there will be shorter periods between fires.

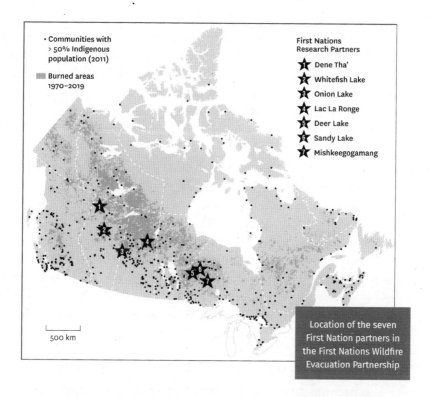

Communities with
> 50% Indigenous
population (2011)

Burned areas
1970–2019

First Nations
Research Partners

⭐ Dene Tha'
⭐ Whitefish Lake
⭐ Onion Lake
⭐ Lac La Ronge
⭐ Deer Lake
⭐ Sandy Lake
⭐ Mishkeegogamang

500 km

Location of the seven
First Nation partners in
the First Nations Wildfire
Evacuation Partnership

Many First Nations are at risk from the effects of wildfire because of their location. But other factors connected to their history of colonization make them more susceptible to the impacts of natural hazards in general:

- *physical factors:* substandard housing and lack of evacuation plans and routes
- *social factors:* lower education levels, chronic health issues, and overcrowding
- *economic factors:* few paid work or business opportunities in communities.

Organizations that keep statistics on Indigenous Peoples such as Statistics Canada, the Assembly of First Nations, and the First Nations Information Governance Centre report that housing crises occur on many reserves because of chronic underfunding by the federal government. Many residents live in homes that are built of substandard materials and suffer from mould issues, and because there are not enough homes to go around, homes are often overcrowded. Many reserves have only one access road, and some have none, which means that when wildfires force evacuations, residents must leave via boat or aircraft.

First Nations communities tend to be quite young, with young children outnumbering Elders. Education and income levels are generally low and unemployment rates high, trends that result in "poverty" in the Western sense. Many adults have not completed high school, and some reserves do not have in-class schooling options for all grades. In many cases, students can go to a local community elementary or middle school, but students who wish to attend high school may need to enroll in online distance-education programs or spend the school year living outside their community in a town or city with a high school. Chronic health issues are also common. First Nations have high rates of chronic diseases, such as heart disease, diabetes, and respiratory conditions.

Indigenous Peoples object when the term "vulnerable" is used to describe them. They feel that this word stigmatizes and overlooks their strength as peoples who have withstood centuries of colonial policies intended to destroy their cultures. Colonial governments and some non-Indigenous researchers employ the term in studies that emphasize the weaknesses caused by colonialism rather than Indigenous Peoples' resilience. For example, many First Nations used to practise cultural burning; they used fire to manage natural resources and to reduce the impact of wildfire on their communities. Today, however, most aren't allowed to burn in their Traditional Territories because of government fire-suppression regulations. Many statistics also reflect Western sensibilities regarding what is valuable in society. If Indigenous Peoples can live successfully off the land, does it matter if they have a high school diploma? Would having a high school diploma lessen the impact of wildfire? Not likely.

The Boreal Forest's Wildfire Cycle

The forest that breathes life into many First Nations is the boreal. If you've spent time deep in the boreal forest in the winter, you know it's a place that may seem barren but is in fact teeming with life, sustaining generations of people. During the winter, as cold temperatures and snow blanket most of Canada, the forest sleeps. The days are short, sometimes lasting only a few hours. In northern Plains Cree, also known as Y-dialect, the month of December is known as pawācakinasīsipīsim (the frost-exploding moon), a time when the trees crackle with cold. It is a time of rest, but this rest is needed because the remainder of the year will be a busy time. When the cold lifts, the boreal forest springs to life as the water runs, the birds return from the south, and the leaves bud. When the forest awakens, so too does wildfire.

The boreal forest regenerates itself through fire. It needs to burn to stay healthy and grow. Pine cones pop open with the heat, releasing seeds that create new forest. In the absence of fire, the boreal forest becomes old and fuel-loaded. Animals have a hard time moving around. Ungulates such as deer, elk, and moose cannot find the fresh young grass they need to put on weight in the summer. This impacts the rest of the food chain.

Fires are necessary, but when they happen, they can be intense and damaging. Although most people think the most dangerous times for wildfire is during the summer, another dangerous period occurs in the spring, generally in May. This time is known as the spring dip, a time when vegetation greens up but the moisture content is at its lowest.

By raising the voices of evacuees, we draw attention to chronic, recurring issues that occur during wildfire evacuations. More important, we present positive examples of what First Nations have done, are doing, and can do to reduce the impact of wildfires on their members. Our case studies demonstrate that external agencies must take a community's context into account in any evacuation plan. For example, a fly-in community will have a different experience leaving via Hercules aircraft than will a First Nation evacuating by road. Their experiences provide a good foundation on which to build recommendations for effective, seamless evacuations that place as little stress on residents as possible.

Cultural Burning

Indigenous Nations have lived sustainably in what is now Canada since time immemorial – for as long as their stories can remember. Indigenous Peoples used fire as a tool to help them manage their territories – to ensure that the ecosystems they lived in could sustain their communities. Many Elders from Indigenous Nations across Canada refer to using fire as "cleaning" the forest. Fire knowledge holders from the community would generally set fires of low intensity during the early spring or late fall, when the fire risk is low. These fires burned deadfall or overgrown underbrush, returning nutrients to the earth, which in turn promoted the quick growth of new grass, berry bushes, and medicinal plants. By reducing some of the fuel load, these fires ensured that fires that started in higher hazard periods (such as on a hot summer day) would have less fuel to burn, rendering them less likely to get out of control.

Community Spotlight

Whitefish Lake First Nation 459, Alberta

In May 2011, the Utikuma Complex Fires caused the evacuation of Whitefish Lake First Nation 459, which is located in north-central Alberta. The main reserve, Utikoomak Lake 155, spreads over 6,756 hectares and has two main settlement areas at Atikameg and Whitefish River. The reserve, located about one hour northeast of the more well-known community of Slave Lake, is accessible by Highway 750 and the Bicentennial Highway (AB-88). Two beautiful lakes – Utikuma Lake, located on the southeast border of the reserve, and the smaller Utikumasis Lake, immediately to the west – offer opportunities for subsistence and recreational activities. The surrounding forest is primarily deciduous, but there are pockets of thick spruce and pine throughout the territory. As in other First Nations communities, the spring dip can be a worrisome time when residents are on the lookout for wildfire.

Whitefish Lake has roughly 2,700 registered band members, and about 1,200 of them live on reserve. More than half of the population speaks Cree at home. The unemployment rate is high – around 35 percent – and income levels are considerably lower than the provincial average. Despite these challenges, the First Nation recently opened a stunning new school, Atikameg, which is K–12 and hosts about two hundred students from Whitefish Lake and nearby Gift Lake Métis Settlement. Fishing and hunting remain important activities in the community.

When wildfire threatened the community in 2011, the evacuation lasted two weeks for most evacuees and three weeks for pregnant women, families with babies, and residents with pre-existing health issues. No lives or homes were lost, but the community suffered significant damage to its infrastructure, including its water and sewage plants.

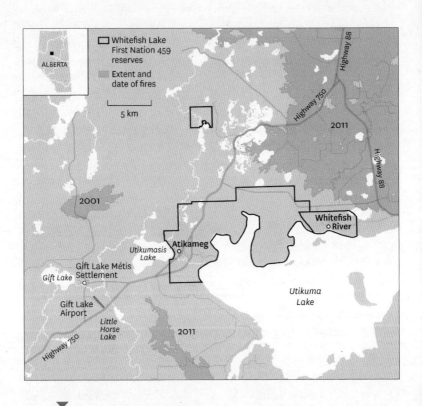

Map legend:
☐ Whitefish Lake First Nation 459 reserves
▨ Extent and date of fires

ALBERTA

5 km

Highway 88

Highway 750

2011

Highway 88

2001

Whitefish River

Atikameg

Utikumasis Lake

Gift Lake Métis Settlement

Gift Lake

Gift Lake Airport

Little Horse Lake

Highway 750

2011

Utikuma Lake

▼

The Utikuma Complex Fires burned
close to the communities of Whitefish
Lake and Atikameg, and damaged
important infrastructure.

1.

DECIDING TO EVACUATE

In the beginning there wasn't any ... Nobody came around to tell us, "Hey, this is serious!" We had to go outside and see it – the cloud of smoke – and it wasn't just the cloud; it's the colour of it. It was looking red and fiery. But it was pretty intense. Just the way it looked.

—COMMUNITY MEMBER, WHITEFISH LAKE FIRST NATION

IN 2011, WHITEFISH Lake First Nation 459 (see spotlight, page 11) residents knew a fire was burning nearby because they could smell the smoke and see ash falling. But they understood that wildfires are a fairly regular occurrence in the summer, so they were not overly concerned. When the next day brought high winds and more smoke and ash, their anxiety heightened; they knew the wind could make the fire spread in their direction in an instant. A band councillor contacted an Alberta government wildfire-management employee, who suggested an evacuation. Since the Chief was out of the community, the councillor consulted by phone and then started the evacuation process.

Each time a First Nation experiences a wildfire near its community, residents face the potential for an evacuation. Not knowing if or when a state of emergency and evacuation will be called only enhances their stress and anxiety. Chiefs and councils, along with the local emergency responders they consult, face tremendous pressure when they are forced to decide whether to call an evacuation, and the community can face tremendous stress if the Chief or council is not available. Often, the lack of full-time emergency managers and comprehensive emergency plans means that First Nations respond in a reactionary way to the wildfire event, and there is often confusion about who is responsible for making the final decision to evacuate. This chapter clears up uncertainty surrounding the detection and decision-making process by outlining how they unfold in both theory and practice.

Fire Detection

Band members typically detect fires or smoke as they go about their day-to-day business. Because of the remoteness and small size of many First Nations communities, they – rather than a police force, forestry service, or wildfire agency – are often responsible for keeping an eye on things. For many northern communities, wildfire or smoke sightings can occur multiple times a summer because of the frequency of fires in the boreal forest. It's difficult to know when one of these wildfires can become a threat to the community, and responding in an appropriate way isn't always as straightforward as it was at Whitefish Lake in 2011.

An ominous cloud of smoke towers over the community of Stanley Mission. *Photos: Lynn Roberts* (left and bottom right); *Vicki Hardlotte* (top right)

14

Some communities, such as Whitefish Lake, spot a fire and evacuate quickly, often within hours. Others watch the fire and smoke linger for weeks as the weather changes and the winds shift direction, driving fire closer to or farther away from the community. In July 2011, many First Nations in northwestern Ontario were threatened by multiple fires. By July 6, several First Nations – including Deer Lake (see spotlight, page 67) – had declared a state of emergency. By contrast, Sandy Lake (see spotlight, page 103), located seventy kilometres north of Deer Lake, did not consider the wildfires an immediate threat. Many residents later reported that they'd noticed fire activity and smoke for about two weeks before the evacuation.

At Mishkeegogamang Ojibway Nation, also located in northwestern Ontario (see spotlight, page 83) residents were aware of the Sioux Lookout Fire 35 for one to two weeks before they were forced to evacuate. From the community, some could see the smoke, and then, as one resident recalled, it was out of control:

> It was right across here, actually, where the fire started. We saw it, too, for days ... It started small from a distance. It started getting bigger and bigger. They hoped that it would burn itself out. So, it just kept getting bigger and bigger until it was out of control ... It wasn't smoky at first, 'cause it was in the distance. You could actually see it growing, getting stronger.

Other residents said that people were concerned but did not know what was going to happen: "There was a lot of talk going around about – you know how it is – a bunch of talk about everything. Some people were saying we were getting ... evacuated, and some people were saying we weren't. We'd ask questions to the leadership, and they wouldn't really answer us 'cause they didn't know much too."

The Decision-Making Process

In First Nations communities, the decision to evacuate ultimately rests with the Chief and band council. In Canada, evacuation orders made by external agencies and provincial emergency-management laws governing mandatory evacuations do not apply to reserve land unless the Chief and council sign a resolution. The police or other agencies cannot legally remove residents who refuse to comply.

The decision to evacuate is never made lightly, and it's never straightforward. But it typically unfolds in three stages:

1   Assessing the risk to the health and safety of band members
2   Consulting with outside agencies
3   Determining the nature and scope of the situation.

Fire and the Right to Self-Determination

In summer 2017, wildfires in British Columbia burned over 1.2 million hectares of land, and 65,000 people were ordered to evacuate. In the central region, Tŝilhqot'in communities were affected by the massive Hanceville and Plateau Fires. Their case received extensive media coverage, not because a First Nation was being threatened by a wildfire but because the Tl'etinqox (Anaham) Government, one of the Tŝilhqot'in communities, refused to issue an evacuation order, the first to do so in Canada. Instead, community members stayed behind to fight the wildfires. Police and other external agencies threatened to remove children, but the First Nation stood by their resolution to look after themselves.

It's important for external agencies to keep in mind that the evacuation process is particularly troubling for First Nations because of Canada's history of colonial policies and practices such as removing Indigenous children from their families and communities. Tl'etinqox had experienced an evacuation in 2010, during which residents had to sleep on cots, were fed non-traditional foods, and were treated with mistrust by staff. The attempted evacuation of Tl'etinqox First Nation and threats to remove children in 2017 brought the trauma associated with residential schools and the Sixties Scoop to the fore. The Nation also knew they had the strength, knowledge, and resilience to control the fires and protect the community on their own. The Tŝilhqot'in Government released a report titled "Nagwediʔk'an gwaneŝ gangu ch'inidʔed ganexwilagh (The Fires Awakened Us): Tsilhqot'in Report – 2017 Wildfires," which details their experiences.

Assessing Risk

It's often difficult for Chiefs and councils to assess risk because the course of a wildfire cannot be predicted. Many factors can influence how fast and where a wildfire grows, including weather, vegetation, drought, and human activities such as fire suppression. The number one concern is human safety. Often, leaders must make this decision without the help of scientific information or outside experts, particularly if multiple communities are being evacuated. For example, in Canada, evacuations because of smoke are generally called when particulate matter ($PM_{2.5}$) in the air exceeds 28 µg/m³, the daily average the government of Canada has deemed safe for humans. However, remote First Nations communities do not have active air-quality monitors; therefore, the decision to evacuate must be based on personal observations. How far can I see? Does it seem bad? Is it hard to breathe?

Sometimes, the risk will become immediately apparent. In 2012 in Saskatchewan, for example, the Harlan Fire started on May 13, posing a threat to Mennonite farms and the Onion Lake Cree Nation, located near the Alberta-Saskatchewan border, fifty kilometres north of Saskatchewan (see spotlight, page 121). On the first day, a few residents at Onion Lake became aware that a wildfire was burning when they saw a large smoke column and heard planes. Most drove toward the smoke to investigate and determined that the risk wasn't too bad. But the next day the wind shifted direction, and the fire threatened their homes. The following spring, the Montanaville Fire came up quickly with no warning. One Elder recalled: "The teenage boys I take care of came running up and told me, 'Grandma, there's a big fire coming fast.' So, I got up and walked out there on the porch. Sure enough, the fire was just red and just blaze flying, coming toward our house, just straight to our house."

Complications Surrounding Jurisdiction

On May 21, 2018, a human-caused wildfire began near Little Grand Rapids First Nation in Manitoba and spread quickly. Being a fly-in community, they requested an evacuation from Indigenous Services Canada, who in turn contacted Manitoba Sustainable Development (the provincial wildfire agency). However, officials from Sustainable Development were unable to reach the Chief and council.

The following day, conditions deteriorated further, with ash falling in the community. The First Nation reached out again to Indigenous Services Canada that afternoon, but there was still confusion, and the evacuation didn't begin until the next evening. By then, smoke was heavy, and only sixty-three high-risk residents were able to be evacuated, as planes couldn't land. The rest stayed in the community gymnasium, which had sprinklers but was filled with smoke.

The next day, six hundred residents were evacuated. The remaining eight hundred evacuated over the next few days. The province released a statement contending that the communities had made the decision to evacuate in consultation with external agencies but that the Chief then announced the evacuation without consulting the province. The leadership of Little Grand Rapids First Nation argued that they had followed what they thought was the proper procedure by contacting the federal agency.

As this example shows, stress and confusion during an evacuation can be amplified by complications surrounding jurisdiction. It is fortunate that no lives were lost because of the fire; however, eleven homes were destroyed.

Whether the threat is distant or immediate, band members will be worried, and they will phone or text the Chief and council, putting added pressure on community leaders to make a decision. Some band members may decide to leave the community on their own before an evacuation has been ordered.

A skimmer tries to douse a wildfire with water near Stanley Mission.
Photo: *Isabelle Hardlotte*

Consulting with External Agencies

Provided there is time, the Chief or council will consult with outside agencies at the local, provincial, and federal levels. In 2011 at Whitefish Lake, for example, many band members were out on the land undertaking traditional summer activities such as hunting, fishing, and berry picking at the time of the wildfires. One of these families included a council member who witnessed a second fire start as a tree fell on a power line. The family hurried to a place with cell reception, and the councillor called a local wildfire ranger from Gift Lake. Because of increased smoke, community concerns about fires approaching their homes, and a shift in the wind's direction, the provincial wildfire-management agency contacted the councillor an hour later and suggested an evacuation. Because the Chief was several hours away in Edmonton, the councillor began the process of evacuating the community.

In 2014, when the Lac La Ronge Indian Band, Stanley Mission (hereafter "Stanley Mission," see spotlight, page 47), was evacuated in north-central Saskatchewan due to the Lagoon Fire, the consultation and decision-making process involved more parties. The wildfire event began when community members sighted numerous smoke columns close by. Rumours flew that an evacuation was imminent. One fire was put out, but a second threatened road access into and out of the community, which meant that an evacuation was needed. Chief and council held a meeting and decided to call an evacuation for this reason. One resident recalled the meeting:

> We went there, and we met with the resources – the firefighters and stuff – and they kept us in contact, like how close the fire was. Our community wasn't really in danger, but our road was. Once the fire reached the road, then there'd be no way in and out, and there'd be heavy smoke. I don't know if they would have been able to bring all the planes in to evacuate people.

When the Lagoon Fire threatened Stanley Mission's only access road, the Chief and council called for a full evacuation. *Photo: Larry Fremont, Government of Saskatchewan*

The entire community was evacuated as the provincial wildland firefighting agency worked to suppress the wildfire. Wildfire mitigation work that had been conducted to the west of the community allowed the fire crews to stop the fire from entering the community.

When it comes to the consultation process, all First Nations can receive information about smoke impacts from Health Canada, although it is difficult to know who to contact during an emergency. Each province or territory has its own agreements, legislation, and policies that influence how it provides support to a First Nation during a wildfire evacuation. Chiefs and band councils should know which external agencies to consult and which regional fire centre they are in, and everyone involved should be familiar with the protocols of their province or territory. It is vital that communities establish relationships with

- regional fire-centre staff
- regional emergency-management representatives
- local mayors, reeves, and municipal officials
- local fire departments of neighbouring communities
- and the police.

Evacuations may be recommended by provincial emergency-operations centres (external agencies involved in fire response and emergency management will have representatives there); however, it is ultimately up to the Chief to order the evacuation.

Determining the Nature and Scope of the Situation
During consultations, Chief and council may decide that the threat to health and well-being does not yet warrant an evacuation order. In these cases, they have two choices:

- *Issue an evacuation alert.* An evacuation alert warns community members that an evacuation order may be coming. It lets them know there is no need to leave the community but advises them to keep an eye on updates and conditions and to begin to prepare.

- *Call a voluntary evacuation.* In this situation, residents can decide whether they wish to stay or leave.

However, once it's determined that the risks to the health and safety of the community are high enough to warrant a mandatory evacuation, the Chief must declare a state of emergency. A mandatory evacuation can't be called without this action, which also triggers the ability to obtain emergency funding from provincial or federal coffers, depending on the agreement. One Chief explained that they had not been aware of this at the time of their wildfire:

> I think communication needs to be clear. For us, we want to be sure who makes that decision. I did not fully understand at the beginning ... It would have been good if somebody would have told me, "You are the Chief. Here is the process. What would happen is we [the Ministry of Natural Resources and Forestry] made the recommendation, and you [the Chief] make the final decision." I wish somebody had told me that, but that did not happen. It was implied. In the end, I found out, but I wish I had been told right from the beginning, right up the front. I wish somebody had said, "The first thing is you have to declare a state of emergency, and then we start working with you, and then we would advise you, and then you make the final decision." If somebody had taken twenty seconds to tell me that, it would have saved me a big headache. But nobody had told me that. So, clear communication up front is very important. It is a good process, but it needs to be communicated.

> Once it is determined that the risks to the health and safety of the community warrant a mandatory evacuation, the Chief must declare a state of emergency.

Once a state of emergency is called, the Chief and council must then decide whether to issue a partial evacuation order for those residents at high risk from smoke or a full evacuation order for all community members. By law, however, band members cannot be forcibly removed from their homes during an evacuation order.

- *Partial evacuation order* (sometimes called Stage 1): A partial evacuation applies either to a specific area of the reserve or a specific group of people, such as the most vulnerable.
- *Full evacuation order* (sometimes called Stage 2): A full evacuation applies to all community members.

A partial evacuation can turn into a full evacuation in the blink of an eye. For example, as mentioned, in 2011 the Chief of Sandy Lake First Nation announced a partial evacuation as wildfires began to advance on the west side of the community. During the partial evacuation, approximately 950 residents at high risk from smoke – people with health issues, disabilities, expectant mothers, Elders, and families with very young children – were evacuated. As one resident recalled, as the smoke settled in Sandy Lake, there was concern about smoke inhalation by those with health problems such as asthma:

> When we had that evacuation some years ago, we had to be flown out because of, health-wise, people have asthma or they can't stand the smell of the smoke ... There's a lot of people that have asthma – the young people, even kids that have asthma, and the elderly. So those are the ones that are taken out first.

Two days later, the Chief announced a full community evacuation because of the increasing proximity of the wildfires and substantially reduced air quality. One resident recalled:

> First we did a partial Stage 1. I think it was five planes that went. The Elders, people with chronic conditions, kids with

high risk, prenatals, children under one. And then the fire kept getting closer, so we had team meetings. We updated each other. Eventually, the fire was nine kilometres away, and it was heading toward the airport. The fire was nine kilometres west of the airport. That was very close. At that time, they decided for a full evacuation. Because if the wind came there, it would just come toward the airport, and you cannot get people out of ... We would all be smoked in. You see, you have got to think about those things. If there is no airport, there is no way you can get people out.

Once a mandatory evacuation is ordered, numerous organizations may be called in to assist with the evacuation, including police, nongovernmental organizations, aid organizations such as the Red Cross, the federal and provincial governments, and host communities. Most important, the community should be informed in the most efficient way possible.

Informing the Community

First Nations communities often don't have a systematic plan for letting the community know about an evacuation order. Residents often hear about the evacuation from various sources, and some don't hear about it at all. And even when the word does get out, confusion often reigns. *Where to go? What should we bring? How long? Who will pay?* To decrease the level of confusion, evacuation orders should be communicated in both English and in the local Indigenous language so that that all residents can understand the order.

At Deer Lake, the majority of residents received information about their evacuation through the community TV station, which broadcast the Chief's announcement. Residents recalled that they heard about the evacuation from family members and friends after the broadcast:

It's usually word of mouth, but usually there will be people at the TV station. They go in front of a camera; they announce these evacuations may happen at this certain time. I heard pretty much word of mouth 'cause, if I'm out in the field, then cellphones didn't really work too good during the first evacuation. But not everybody had a cellphone. But it was just word of mouth.

At Sandy Lake, the majority of residents received information about the evacuation through community radio. Others heard through word of mouth from family and community members, social media such as Facebook, and the local police.

In some cases, though, none of these methods worked. At Onion Lake, some community members did not hear about the evacuation until someone came to their door. One resident recalled:

The ones that talked to me were security. [They] told us to prepare for evacuation because ... And by then the fire was just across the road, and it was smoky. It was smoky in here, and I guess it jumped across the road. There was choppers here, bombers, everything. It's like a war zone, and they drove in. They told us we had to leave.

At Mishkeegogamang, where the evacuation was carried out over three days, the Chief announced the evacuation order and evacuation plans on the local radio station. Residents in general had adequate time to prepare; however, those who were outside the community were not notified immediately, if at all. One resident found out about the evacuation only when he tried to return home and was turned back at the barricades. A group of residents who lived in and around Pickle Lake were not informed about the evacuation until a Pickle Lake resident stepped in to ensure that they were provided with food and accommodation.

When Whitefish Lake was evacuated, residents were confused about what was going on. Some residents had a few hours to get ready to evacuate; others had fifteen minutes to prepare; while still others found out about the evacuation only when the police came to their door and told them to leave immediately. One resident recalled:

At first, we didn't know what was going on 'cause there was a whole bunch of people driving erratically around, and we didn't know what was going on. And there was ashes coming from above. I thought that this was just a normal grass fire. So we didn't know. I had my grandchildren with me, my brother. And we didn't even know anything was going on until someone came and told us, "Are you guys gonna leave? 'Cause the fire is not too far, and we have to evacuate ... You guys were supposed to leave a long time ago." "Why? What for?" And then the fire's coming this way. We didn't know. Nobody alarmed us about it until they came along and told us that we had to evacuate.

Others were concerned about how little information they had received once they were told to evacuate:

You don't have to panic. Explain to them the best thing to do instead of saying, "We gotta leave right now" ... They should have explained it and tell them instead of scaring them. You know that's scary – somebody to come and tell you there's fire not far from here, pack up and go ... How far is that fire? You wanna know.

As these examples show, having an evacuation plan that includes how to inform residents about local conditions and the decision to stay or evacuate is of vital importance.

Guiding Questions for First Nations

- Do you have a clear idea of the local, provincial, and federal agencies you should consult with if there is a wildfire? Do you have contact information for current staff? Do they have your up-to-date contact information?
- Do you understand the steps that need to be taken to call an evacuation and the options that are open to you?
- Do you understand the funding arrangements in your province or territory?

Community radio stations, like this one at Mishkeegogamang Ojibway Nation, are vital sources of information before and during evacuations.
Photo: Tara McGee

- Is there a plan for how you will communicate an evacuation order to members? Is there a specific person who will be assigned this role? Are community members aware of this arrangement? What about community members who may not have access to radio or the internet? What about community members who are outside the community at the time of the evacuation? If door-to-door announcements are part of the plan, are the people responsible for contacting residents trained? Do they have the correct facts and information to relay to residents? Are there plans to ensure that the evacuation order is also communicated in your local language?

Guiding Questions for External Agencies
- Are you reaching out to First Nations annually in your area to ensure they have current contact information? Do you know how to contact the Chief or the emergency manager?

- Are you sharing real-time information with the community about wildfires and predictions about fire growth?
- Are you being transparent with the First Nation on decisions being made on your side? For example, how are you suppressing fires? What information do you consider when you decide to recommend an evacuation?

Community Spotlight

Dene Tha' (/'dɛnɛ ðaː/) First Nation, Taché, Alberta

The community of Taché is located in the northwestern corner of Alberta, near the town of High Level, just over 100 kilometres from the Northwest Territories. It is part of the Dene Tha' First Nation, which in Dene Dhah means "the people common to the territory" or "common peoples." The majority of the Dene Tha' inhabit three of seven reserves. The three reserves, in order of most to least populated, are Chateh (formerly known as Assumption), Bushe River, and Taché. The latter's anglicized name is Meander River, given to it because of its spectacular location overlooking the confluence of the Meander and Hay Rivers. The reserve covers 1,418 hectares located in the heart of the boreal forest. Deciduous trees such as aspen, poplar, and willow abound, making the time known as the spring dip particularly dangerous for this community.

Taché has a population of approximately four hundred people, many of whom live in multigenerational homes. Its band complex houses a radio station, a health centre, a school (K–9), community services such as counselling and social work, and a small volunteer fire department. Although these services employ a few people, employment opportunities in the community are scarce. Community members maintain their livelihood from a combination of wage work, government subsidies, and traditional subsistence activities such as fishing, trapping, and hunting. But the community is young – the average age is twenty-six. Like other First Nations in Canada, Taché is subject to socio-economic challenges.

In July 2012, heavy wildfire smoke from the Lutose Complex Fire led to an evacuation that lasted for one week. The wildfire caused no damage to community houses or buildings, and no one was seriously injured. But the residents' lives were severely disrupted because they had little time to prepare and were unfamiliar with evacuation processes. Despite these and other significant issues, the community managed to use local personnel and resources to carry out the evacuation with little outside assistance.

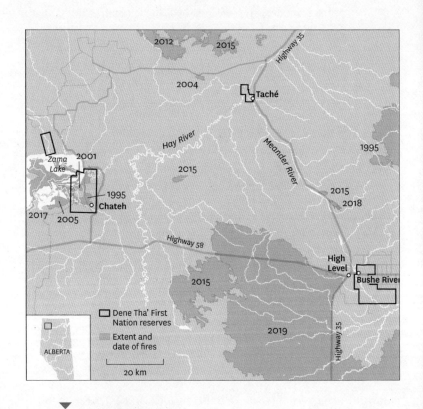

In recent years, several wildfires
have burned close to Dene Tha' First
Nation's three main communities:
Taché (Meander River), Chateh
(Assumption), and Bushe River.

2.

PUTTING A PLAN IN MOTION

We were puttin' the kids to sleep, and everybody had pyjamas on. And
then somebody bang on my door real hard, and I was wondering, *What's
goin' on?* So, I opened the door, and they said you got fifteen minutes to
get everything you need and to meet us at the band office for evacuation.
—COMMUNITY MEMBER, DENE THA' FIRST NATION, TACHÉ

IN JULY 2012, the volunteer fire chief of the Dene Tha' First Nation
community of Taché, located in northwestern Alberta (see spotlight, page 29), became concerned about the deteriorating air quality
caused by the heavy wildfire smoke from the Lutose Complex Fire.
He asked the director of emergency management for the Nation to
come to Taché. After driving 100 kilometres from Chateh, the director judged the severity of the air conditions using personal observations rather than an air-quality monitor, which was not available.
She immediately called for a voluntary evacuation of residents at
high-risk from smoke: small children, infants, pregnant women,
people with chronic respiratory problems, and Elders. The evacuation began at approximately 9:00 p.m. and continued until the following morning.

To carry out the partial evacuation, the emergency director followed a generic emergency plan provided by the Alberta Emergency
Management Agency that had not been formally tailored to Dene Tha'
First Nation or its three main communities. No residents had been
assigned the task of assisting during the evacuation, and the plan did
not contain a list of high-risk residents or maps of where they lived.
In the absence of this information, the director and the volunteer
fire chief relied on their personal knowledge of the residents and the

31

Sunlight filtering through thick smoke casts an eerie glow over the community of Taché.
Photo: Sid Chambaud

generic emergency plan to carry out the evacuation. They asked volunteers to go door to door to spread the word. Unfamiliar with evacuation procedures, the volunteers meant well but confused residents by failing to relay important information such as the location of the fire, what to pack, where to go, and the partial and voluntary nature of the evacuation. Due in part to this lack of communication, most of Taché's four hundred residents chose to evacuate. Family members in multigenerational households, which was most of the community, also wanted to accompany and support their loved ones.

Several hours after the voluntary evacuation began, the air quality visibly deteriorated. At this stage, the Chief, who had been on the way to Edmonton when the evacuation began, arrived in Taché. Following consultation with the emergency director, the Chief declared a local state of emergency followed by a mandatory evacuation order. But by that time, most of the community had already left.

As this example suggests, once an evacuation is ordered, a number of things should happen:

- Each First Nation should have an assigned emergency manager, whether volunteer or paid, and an emergency plan.
- Assistance from federal, provincial, and nongovernmental organizations (e.g., the Red Cross) should be triggered.
- Residents should be told how long they have to prepare, what they should take with them, and where they should go.
- Organizers should understand and know how to deal with people who don't want to leave, and they should know who should stay behind.

These are the things that should happen, but former evacuees often report that their communities were not adequately prepared to deal with the emergency situation. By systematically exploring the problems they encountered, this chapter lays the groundwork for constructing an evacuation plan and putting an evacuation in motion.

The Emergency Manager and Plan

In 2013, when the Auditor General of Canada released its audit of emergency management on First Nations reserves (see the emergency preparedness sidebar in the Introduction on pages 2–3), the report confirmed that some First Nations were not well prepared for emergencies. The report found that some communities had no plans for managing emergencies and that the plans that did exist were outdated and often incomplete.

> Some First Nations have no plans for managing emergencies, and the plans that they do have are often outdated or incomplete.

None of the seven partner First Nations had a full-time emergency manager responsible for preparing and updating plans, ensuring the preparedness of local residents, and carrying out other emergency-management activities. The person responsible for emergency management was often employed full-time in another position and carried out the emergency-manager role in a voluntary, part-time capacity. The director of emergency management at Dene Tha', for example, also served as a health coordinator. At Whitefish Lake and Mishkeegogamang Ojibway First Nations, the volunteer emergency manager also looked after public works. Part of the problem is that Indigenous Services Canada does not directly provide money to bands for an emergency-manager position. Instead, each band must decide to use core funding on emergency management, at the expense of other programs.

Only a few of the First Nations had an up-to-date emergency plan tailored to their communities. Stanley Mission, Onion Lake, and Deer Lake had emergency plans, but the latter's did not include a list of high-risk residents. Although Dene Tha' and Whitefish Lake only had the generic emergency plan developed by the Alberta Emergency Management Agency, the plan was more useful than having no plan at all, which was the situation at Mishkeegogamang and Sandy Lake.

The experiences of Deer Lake, which had to complete two partial evacuations of people at high risk from wildfire smoke in July 2011, reveal the importance of having a complete up-to-date emergency plan. Because there was no evacuation plan in place during the first partial evacuation, the Chief, band councillors, and nurses had to quickly prepare a list of residents who needed to be evacuated first. The time they spent preparing the list meant they had less time to organize these people's medical records before they left. They also had little time to arrange for community liaisons to go with these evacuees or to ensure that the residents had a caregiver or family member to accompany them. Without these sources of support, already vulnerable residents had a more traumatic evacuation experience.

Identifying High-Risk Residents

When a Chief or council orders a partial evacuation, they indicate whether a specific part of the community or certain groups of high-risk residents must leave. High-risk individuals are typically Elders and fragile people who

- have health conditions exacerbated by smoke (pregnant women, children under two, Elders, and people with heart or lung diseases)
- need assistance with mobility
- need home care or an escort
- may have no mobility and need a high level of care
- may need to be admitted to hospital.

An evacuation plan should include contact information for these individuals and their caregivers. With this information, emergency managers and staff can contact them as quickly as possible and gather medical files for the evacuation. The community should also have a designated wildfire smoke safe haven for residents, a place such as a community hall, school, or other building that includes an air-purification system.

Working with External Agencies and Nongovernmental Organizations

When an evacuation is ordered, a number of external agencies and nongovernmental organizations will be triggered to help deal with the emergency. However, some First Nations may decide to not involve external agencies or organizations. In 2012 and 2013, for instance, when a portion of the Onion Lake Cree Nation in Alberta had to perform a partial evacuation, the community had an emergency plan, but it tried to keep its response internal to avoid the confusion of bringing in outside agencies or organizations. Regardless of a First Nation's location or stance on involving outside agencies, a full emergency plan should include contact information for these agencies and organizations and a rundown of their responsibilities.

As mentioned in the previous chapter, the external agencies involved depend on the province or territory, and the degree of their involvement shifts from province to province. Generally information from various government agencies (like wildfire management or emergency management) is received by the incident management team, who then pass that on to the Chief or local emergency manager. This can include information like predicted fire growth, weather conditions, potential evacuation routes, host communities, and so on. In rapid incidents, often the Chief must make the decision to evacuate based on what they are observing or what is being reported to them locally.

Nongovernmental organizations such as the Red Cross and Salvation Army may be involved in organizing and supporting evacuees. For example, during the evacuation of Stanley Mission, the Red Cross set up and staffed evacuation centres; provided food, donated items, and other essentials; and organized recreation activities for children. Their involvement is often established pre-event through agreements between governmental and nongovernmental agencies.

Having Time to Prepare and Knowing What to Take

Depending on how the fire is detected and how long the consultation takes, the time residents have to prepare to evacuate can vary from a few days to none. When evacuees are given no time to prepare, they experience considerable distress since they must get organized quickly and feel pressured by emergency officials to leave. At Onion Lake Cree Nation in Saskatchewan, residents left immediately once they heard the evacuation order and took only a few things such as a purse with them. Some described seeing flames as they left their homes. They didn't have time to pack and feared their houses would be lost.

One woman said her family left everything behind because her husband refused to leave and remained behind to defend their property. Two residents were forced to leave their pets behind. Families had frightening experiences during the last-minute evacuation. One resident recalled that her husband and his brothers all came rushing over here to grab everything. Fridge and stove, everything, they took it out. That's how fast they were working. Just because they said that it was gonna burn ... I remember, anyways, I seen black smoke, real black smoke, and everybody was saying, "It's your house," and I was crying, and I was telling them, "Don't say that."

As these experiences show, the sooner residents are warned, the better the response, although this is not always possible in sudden wildfire events.

Residents from Whitefish Lake indicated they were told they only had ten to fifteen minutes to leave, which was just enough time to pack a small bag of essentials. This made them feel rushed, panicky, and unprepared – especially because it was late at night. In Taché, the last-minute evacuation combined with a lack of information caused even more stress: "But we really didn't get that much information. What was really goin' on? You know? The main thing was people were worried about their houses and all that because it was such short notice where people had to run around. And they said the fire was just right there. So a lot of people were worried. That's all."

Residents from Sandy Lake, a fly-in community, also said they did not have sufficient time to prepare. Because of this, some residents, including the elderly and those with chronic health issues, failed to bring along essential items, including medication, puffers, money, and identification cards. One resident recalled that

everybody was told to pack at 7:00. We were at the airport by 8:00. By 10:30, we were on the first plane, and before 12:00 we were in Sioux Lookout ... Some evacuees at Stage 1 didn't even take their puffer, or they were out because we were just puffing all the time. Then some of them, they didn't take their insulin because, the night before, we didn't have enough time to go pick up the insulin, so whatever we had, we just packed up and then went.

Taking pets into consideration is an important part of evacuation planning, particularly since pet ownership may influence a resident's willingness to evacuate. For First Nations with road access, evacuees will generally want to take along pets that reside with them in their home, such as dogs or cats. In some cases, they will also want to move horses or other livestock out of harm's way. Care of evacuated animals is now a prominent part of emergency planning. Many evacuation centres and hotels make space for pets, and host communities will often make plans to pasture evacuated livestock.

Evacuation plans should also include caring for pets and animals left behind. Owners may leave them behind because they are outside pets, because the evacuation centre can't accommodate them, or because they were away from home when the evacuation was ordered. Care for these animals is often provided either by those who remain in the community (often as security or essential staff) or by volunteer groups who are allowed to access the community. It is important for volunteers to understand that animals left behind are still wanted. Animals should not be placed for adoption until well after community members have returned home and reunification efforts have been made. During the 2019 wildfire evacuation of Bigstone Cree Nation, for example, Alberta Animal Disaster Response worked with the Nation and the MD of Opportunity/Wabasca to feed and care for animals left behind (the case is documented on the Second Chance Animal Rescue Society's website, scarscare.ca/emergency-wildfire-rescue).

In fly-in communities, residents have no choice but to leave pets and livestock behind, and the ability to bring in outside assistance to look after animals can be limited. Often, those who remain in the community are tasked with feeding and caring for the animals, which may mean accessing evacuees' homes. Caring for the animals also depends on having a stockpile of pet food in the community, something that should be considered in the evacuation plan. During past evacuations, caregivers have posted pictures and videos to social media so owners can see that their pets are being fed.

What Should People Take with Them?

Imagine you are told that you need to leave your home within the next fifteen minutes or a few hours. What would you take? What would you leave behind? Some evacuees remembered taking important items such as insurance papers, medication, and their driver's licence. Others took bags of clothes. One youth took his TV and video game system!

A complete evacuation plan will include instructions for how and when to let people know what to take with them. The instructions should include the following essentials:

- medicine
- wallets and identification
- a change or two of clothing per person.

Seeing to Those Who Remain Behind

During evacuations, individuals in charge of essential services, with approval of the Chief, will remain behind if they can. At Mishkee-gogamang and Sandy Lake in Ontario, the Chiefs and key staff remained behind to

- look after infrastructure
- maintain essential services
- provide updates on the fires
- provide information to evacuees
- assist firefighters.

Feeding animals, like these outside dogs at Stanley Mission, is an important job for those who remain behind to maintain essential services.
Photo: Chico Halkett

39

> In Canada, provincial emergency-management laws governing mandatory evacuations do not apply to First Nation reserves. Therefore, the police or other agencies cannot legally remove residents who refuse to comply.

The Chief of Sandy Lake said it was his traditional responsibility as a Chief to protect the community. He also wanted to encourage, motivate, and support residents who stayed behind to secure homes, feed pets, engage in firefighting, or assist firefighters.

Most residents agree to evacuate when they are told to do so, but some may be reluctant to leave. In Canada, provincial emergency-management laws governing mandatory evacuations do not apply to First Nation reserves. Therefore, the police or other external agencies cannot legally remove residents who refuse to comply. First Nations and external agencies should be aware – and respectful – of the reasons people may not want to leave.

A Desire to Protect Homes and Property

A man from the Dene Tha' First Nation community of Taché reported that he had been reluctant to evacuate because he was concerned about leaving his house undefended in case the fire came closer to the community. Likewise, at Mishkeegogamang, a resident with fire-fighter training stayed behind because he thought he might obtain work fighting the fire. He was waiting in line to get on the bus when he made the decision and, indeed, was later recruited for this work.

A resident of Onion Lake also stayed behind to help in the fire-fighting effort because he wanted to save the community's property and protect the area. He recalled: "Wherever we were needed, we went. No front-line firefighting or nothing; we wouldn't have the training for it. But ... if we needed to haul water to the bush or something in tanks ... we'd take those, run to the bush, squirt stuff down,

Wildland firefighters were brought in to battle the flames near Stanley Mission, Saskatchewan.
Photo: Chico Halkett

grab the hose if we needed to, move hoses around. Stuff like that." At Sandy Lake, some residents wanted to remain behind because they thought it was the responsibility of young adults to protect the community: "We thought we were going to be fighting fires, helping out at the front line, or whatever, 'cause that's what we were normally taught to do, I guess you could say. Like, it's our instinct to stay behind and help, because you're a guy, so that's what we thought." This comment reveals the gendered perspectives that often influence evacuation decisions: men often feel like their role is to fight the fire, while women and children are more likely to evacuate.

Whereas some residents might want to stay to help fight the fires, other might want to protect their house or belongings. A woman from Mishkeegogamang, pregnant at the time, explained that she did not want to leave pictures and other precious belongings behind. She left only when the police came to her door. At Sandy Lake, some residents were worried about their houses being broken into. A resident of Whitefish Lake said it was a legitimate concern:

At the start of every evacuation, like last year, there's always hesitation from the community members to leave the community. There's a lot of stubborn community members, that they think their house is gonna get broken into, so they're hesitant to leave. So what they did last year, too, is, well – everybody knows who breaks into the places, so those are the first people they try and get out of here. So that makes the rest of the community very willing to go.

But a group of men did stay behind to protect property during the evacuation. One of them recalled that the police had tried to arrest him but backed off when he said they'd have to arrest all twenty-five men. The men organized themselves into a security team and met each day with the police and a councillor, who brought in gas and food to support their efforts. For fifteen exhausting days, the men drove around, checking on the wildfire, ensuring that residents' homes were secure, and feeding pets. They also became an important source of information for evacuees and helped to dispel rumours.

A community member who stayed behind to fight the fire at Whitefish Lake describes the wildfire. *Photo: Amy Cardinal Christianson*

They Do Not Feel That Their Health or Homes Are at Risk

Alternatively, residents may decide to stay because they don't think their health or homes are at risk. Some residents of Taché, for instance, felt an evacuation was warranted only for those people sensitive to wildfire smoke. Likewise, at Mishkeegogamang, a man thought his house would be protected by sprinkler systems being set up by the Ministry of National Resources and Forestry. He planned to stay behind in his house and would take to the water in his canoe if needed. He left only when a friend who was living in one of the host communities took him away. At Whitefish Lake, some women reported that they had to convince their husbands to leave: "I just packed up my trailer and told my husband to hook it up. And he really didn't wanna leave, 'cause he's just yapping away, 'It's not gonna come here,' and this and that. But I just kept on packing anyway."

Fear of Flying, Fear of Leaving the Community, or Wanting to Retain Control

Indigenous Peoples in isolated communities may not want to evacuate because they fear flying, have never left their community, or simply want to retain a sense of control. A resident of Sandy Lake recalled: "Some community members wanted to stay behind because there are a lot of people in the community where they don't like to fly on the plane. So, that was one of the reasons. I mean, they were scared." At Mishkeegogamang, two residents chose not to evacuate because they rarely left the community. They wanted to feel like they were in control of their own actions and wanted to avoid staying in a place that didn't feel like home. As one male participant explained, "Nobody to tell me what to do, and what time I should go to sleep, and 'Don't go over there,' and so on." These two participants stayed in their cabin in the Traditional Territory.

Despite having legitimate reasons for not wanting to leave, most residents will agree to go if the police come to their door. When police help carry out an evacuation, they may threaten to arrest or charge residents. And, in some cases, residents might assume that they'll be charged if they don't comply with the evacuation order. A resident of Mishkeegogamang said the evacuation reminded her of Indigenous children in Canada being taken away to residential schools: "It made me feel like ... You know when, long time ago, they used to ... the residential [school] thing. That's what it felt like ... Yeah, it felt like that, but with older people though ... Yeah, that's how it felt. You had no choice."

Alternative Evacuation Plans

Finally, some residents have alternative plans, as an evacuee from Sandy Lake explained:

> Me and my father, we wanted to go to our camp up north so we could stay away from the fire. We have our family trapline up north; it's just a boat ride, probably about two and half hour's ride from here. It's near to the Manitoba line border. We would have been safe there, but they wanted everybody out. My mother said, "You guys all go." She's the voice of the family, and we must obey.

Going to a cabin or alternative location can enable residents to stay near their communities and in familiar surroundings. Other evacuees may choose to stay with friends or family who live nearby instead of going to one of the designated host communities.

Emergency planners should take people's alternative plans into consideration. When the fly-in community of Deer Lake was evacuated, for instance, residents who chose to stay were asked to sign a waiver. One man whose family members were on the list to be evacuated with the high-risk group to Smiths Falls signed a waiver so his family would not have to go. He recalled:

> For them to go all the way down to Smith Falls, I did not want at all. They had me sign a waiver. Which I gladly signed. My family's my responsibility is what they told me, and it's always been like that anyways. They're my responsibility. I made those children so. But still I didn't feel regret or anything like that. I thought, and I was happy to have my family here, and, like, I can sleep at night, you know, instead of having to wake up every couple

hours and think, *Are they okay down there? Are they being treated okay?* That put my mind to rest. Like I made the right choice for my family, for me and my family, so I said no. I was pretty happy about my choices.

In addition to having residents who stay behind sign waivers, it's also important that they have all the information, support, resources, and preparedness that they need to stay safe.

Leaving a community that is threatened by a wildfire or smoke is always a difficult, stressful time for both the residents and those organizing the evacuation. When you add in the additional complications of dealing with external agencies, identifying and informing high-risk residents, and balancing the safety of community members with their right to make their own choices, devising and putting an evacuation into action can be a real challenge. Being prepared at all stages is key.

Guiding Questions for First Nations

- Do you have access to funding to hire an emergency manager?
- Do you have an emergency plan? Is it specific to your Nation? Are the external agency contacts up to date?
- Who from your Nation is responsible for making sure the emergency plan is prepared, updated, and followed?
- Is it possible for you to maximize the evacuation warning time, so residents have as much time as possible to prepare?
- Have you identified trigger points around your community – for example, a particular geographic feature, such as a road, that will trigger an evacuation as soon as the wildfire crosses it?
- Are your community members informed about the impacts of wildfire smoke and how to protect their health during a wildfire smoke event?
- Does your community have a list of high-risk residents and a safe haven for them to avoid smoke?
- Can families be kept together during an evacuation so family members can support each other?

- Are community members who stay behind during a wild-fire adequately prepared? Do they have adequate resources to protect their safety?
- Are there places within your Traditional Territory where people can stay during a wildfire if conditions permit? Will they have access to resources to ensure their well-being and safety?
- What community knowledge exists in regard to wildfire and wildfire smoke?
- Do community evacuation plans include a list of community liaisons in case of an evacuation?

Guiding Questions for External Agencies
- Are you allowing the First Nation to take a leadership role in evacuation planning and actual evacuations, as they understand the needs and values of their members?
- Is it possible for First Nations to stay within their Traditional Territory when conditions permit if they have the resources to do this safely, including designated safe havens from wildfire smoke?
- Why do some people not want to leave during a wildfire? Asking this question will help to identify constraints that can be addressed. For example, concerns about the security of homes can be addressed by essential staff who remain behind during a wildfire to provide security.

Community Spotlight

Lac La Ronge Indian Band, Stanley Mission, Saskatchewan

Lac La Ronge Indian Band is located in north-central Saskatchewan and has 10,152 members and twenty reserves. The band's reserves are located within the boreal forest, where there are networks of waterways and lakes that run across the Canadian Shield. Because of the suppression of wildfires, stands of thick black spruce dominate the landscape, placing the territory at constant risk of large wildfires and evacuations. Band members are heavily involved in hunting, fishing, trapping, berry picking, and medicine collecting. Stanley 157, referred to as Stanley Mission, is the most populated of the Lac La Ronge Indian Band reserves, with a population of 1,650. A small non-Indigenous community lies to the north of the reserve. Services in Stanley Mission include an administrative office, community hall, health centre, police station, grocery store, and post office, along with a church, gas stations, restaurants, and schools.

In May 2014, the Lagoon Wildfire that burned near Stanley 157 and the adjacent non-Indigenous community threatened access roads and power lines. Lac La Ronge Indian Band called a partial evacuation and then a full evacuation of the community. Approximately 1,600 residents were sent to Saskatoon, Prince Albert, and La Ronge. The evacuation lasted only a few days, but those at high risk did not return to the community for one week. One year later, in June 2015, a partial evacuation of Stanley Mission was called to remove vulnerable residents because of high levels of wildfire smoke. Some evacuees were out of the community for over three weeks.

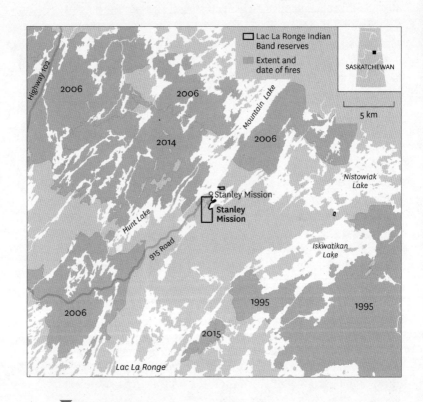

Lac La Ronge Indian
Band reserves

Extent and
date of fires

SASKATCHEWAN

5 km

Highway 102

2006

2006

2006

2014

Mountain Lake

Nistowiak
Lake

Stanley Mission

Stanley
Mission

Hunt Lake

915 Road

Iskwatikan
Lake

2006

1995

1995

2015

Lac La Ronge

When the 2014 Lagoon Fire burned
close to Stanley Mission, community
members evacuated to several
different towns in Saskatchewan.

3.

TROUBLESHOOTING TRANSPORTATION

You didn't know exactly how you were going to move more than 2,700 people in three days.
— COMMUNITY FRONT-LINE WORKER,
SANDY LAKE FIRST NATION, 2011 EVACUATION

IN MAY 2014, when Lac La Ronge Indian Band ordered an evacuation for Stanley Mission, staff at the band office called the various departments (Public Works, the health centre, the school, and so on) to tell them an evacuation order had been issued. Children were either sent home from school by bus, on foot, or their parents came to pick them up. Essential staff – mostly from the band office and health centre – went to the Band Hall to register evacuees as they left the community and to coordinate transportation for those without a vehicle. At first, the evacuation only included children under two (and a parent or other caregiver), people with chronic health conditions, and Elders. Soon after, the evacuation order included the whole community. All residents were asked to go to the Band Hall to register. They also had to indicate whether they would require transportation or could leave in their own vehicle.

Stanley Mission residents found out about the evacuation via radio, door-to-door alerts by the police, and the community siren. Departure times for the buses from the Band Hall were announced over the radio in both English and Cree. Although the evacuation was well organized, a resident recalled that there was misinformation about the evacuation on the local community Facebook page:

Just a lot of misinformation, and as good as Facebook is, in a situation where you have evacuations and you have a situation like that, where it is dire, people need to get the proper information out. There was a lot of misinformed people that were commenting on Facebook. And because of the misinformation that was being passed around, people were unsure where they were supposed to go. That was a problem I noticed last year.

Transportation issues occurred in all of the First Nations showcased here. In the two fly-in communities, Sandy Lake and Deer Lake, residents were uncomfortable with being flown out of their community on large Hercules aircraft. In First Nations with road access such as Stanley Mission and Whitefish, some evacuees either lacked cars or gas or their vehicles were uninsured and unregistered. Many residents had to be picked up by family members or other local residents. Four communities – Mishkeegogamang, Stanley Mission, Dene Tha' (Taché), and Whitefish Lake – arranged for buses to transport evacuees, and the evacuation at Mishkeegogamang went smoothly partly because extra buses happened to be on hand at the time of the evacuation. But at Sandy Lake and Stanley Mission, where multistage evacuations were carried out, residents had to wait for long periods before boarding a bus to their final destination. These Nations' experiences reveal the importance of transportation being organized in advance and vehicles being available so that communities are not left scrambling at the last minute. To troubleshoot transportation issues, it's important to consider whether residents will be evacuating by road or by air and to have a fully developed plan for multistage evacuations. This chapter, by showcasing problems encountered in the past along with success stories, will help you troubleshoot common transportation issues that may arise during a future evacuation.

Transportation by Road
The majority of First Nations in Canada are accessible by road, although for many it is a single gravel road that may be poorly maintained. In the First Nations Wildfire Evacuation Partnership, Taché,

Whitefish Lake, Onion Lake, Stanley Mission, and Mishkeegogamang are all accessible by road. However, community members also use other methods to get around their territory, including off-highway vehicles, boats, and animals (horses, dog sleds). Because of the remote location of many of the communities, the time spent evacuating by road can be anywhere from one hour (Whitefish Lake and Taché) to over twelve hours (Stanley Mission), and the problems that residents encounter in the absence of advance preparation and a well-thought-out plan can include the following:

- lack of vehicles
- gas-related issues
- uncertainty about the destination.

> Every evacuation plan should include alternative transportation plans for residents who don't have access to their own vehicles.

Lack of Vehicles
Every evacuation plan should include alternative transportation plans for residents who don't have access to their own vehicles. For example, at Mishkeegogamang, where buses happened to be on hand for the evacuation, the radio station provided residents with information about how the evacuation would unfold and when buses would pick up residents. Parents were told to keep an eye on children to make sure they could evacuate quickly. Residents at high risk from smoke and band members eager to leave evacuated first. They either took a bus or drove to Sioux Lookout (230 kilometres away). A second group, which included many families with older children, left on the second day by bus to Ignace (263 kilometres away). A third group, composed mainly of people who did not want to leave, were driven to Pickle Lake airport by bus and then flown to Geraldton (763 kilometres away) on the third day.

Emergency Kits
for Buses

If the host community is a long drive away, be sure to advise residents to prepare in advance for the trips and, if possible, have emergency kits on hand for the buses. Although the evacuation of residents from Mishkeegogamang Ojibway Nation, which was carried out over three days, was perceived to be effective, residents were not prepared for the long bus trips to Sioux Lookout and Ignace. One resident recalled: "It was hard because some mothers left with nothing – they didn't leave with no Pampers, nothing. They just got up and left ... That was kind of hard, though, because there was babies crying on the bus. It was hot, and I don't know if anybody had eaten supper ... Yeah, they didn't have stuff to eat all the way there – three hours."

At minimum, emergency kits for buses should include diapers, nonperishable food items, water, and blankets.

At Whitefish Lake, the band likewise organized for school buses to pick up and transport evacuees, but some people were stranded. Some evacuated via the highway on quads. One resident recalled walking down a main road until a resident picked him up; four other stranded residents rode along with him in the back of the truck. Others left in vehicles packed full of people and belongings. Some picked up individuals who they knew didn't have their own vehicle, often an older family member. One grandmother described evacuating in a small pickup truck with her husband, five grandchildren, and their belongings. First Nation households often include more people than can fit legally in one vehicle, and a few residents recalled being nervous about evacuating because they did not want to get tickets or face charges for leaving the reserve in overloaded vehicles.

Residents may have access to a vehicle and gasoline but no licence, insurance, or registration. One evacuee recalled: "I seen policemen and everything everywhere. They were saying to people to grab their cars even if they don't have learners or if their car's not registered, or anything, but just go anyways."

Gas-Related Issues

Alternative transportation plans should ensure that all residents have quick access to gasoline and that there is enough gasoline available in the community to evacuate everyone. At Whitefish, for example, some residents had vehicles but did not have enough gas or money to evacuate. Recognizing this, the Chief and council advised residents through word of mouth to stop at the local gas station to fill up. The gas would be paid for by the band: "We phoned the Chief. We told him what's going on, and he said, 'Go to the store and gas up everybody and ship out to High Prairie.' He was gonna call around for the hotels for people."

Although this seemed like a sound plan, the directive resulted in a long line of evacuees at the gas station. Participants who had not heard about the free gas through word of mouth joined the line when they noticed it as they drove down the main highway. The gas quickly ran out. One resident recalled: "We tried [to get some gas], but they had already run out at the time."

Uncertainty about the Destination

Once residents are gassed up, they need to know where to go. At Whitefish, residents were not sure where to go, so many drove to the town of High Prairie (92 kilometres away) either because it was the closest community or because they were simply following others. At High Prairie, they were told to head to the arena to register for hotels. But because the hotels were also accommodating evacuees from nearby Gift Lake Métis Settlement, some people couldn't find a room. They had to drive 90 kilometres southwest to Valleyview, and a few had to continue a further 112 kilometres to Grande Prairie to find accommodation. Some Elders had language difficulties when they arrived in High Prairie and did not understand what they were supposed to do. One couple ended up sleeping in their car for the first night of the evacuation and then drove to stay with friends.

At Taché, residents without vehicles were told by the director of emergency management, the volunteer fire chief, family members, and other community residents to gather at the band complex, where

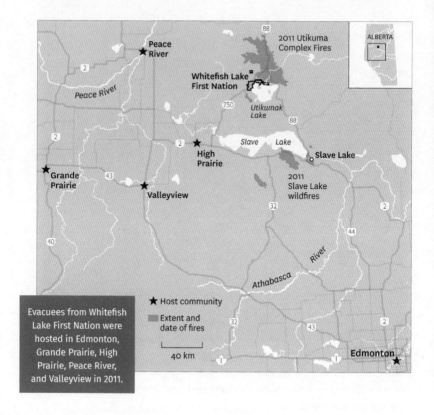

Peace
River

2011 Utikuma
Complex Fires

ALBERTA

Whitefish Lake
First Nation

Peace River

Utikumak
Lake

Slave   Lake

High
Prairie

Slave Lake

Grande
Prairie

2011
Slave Lake
wildfires

Valleyview

River

Athabasca

★ Host community

Extent and
date of fires

40 km

Edmonton

Evacuees from Whitefish
Lake First Nation were
hosted in Edmonton,
Grande Prairie, High
Prairie, Peace River,
and Valleyview in 2011.

a charter bus would transport them to a reception centre at High Level. The number of evacuees requiring transportation exceeded capacity, so the bus made two trips. Those who had their own vehicles didn't know where to go, so most headed to High Level. Only a few went straight to the official community-run reception centre at the band complex in Bushe River, located just east of High Level. Confusion stemmed from the fact that a simultaneous evacuation was taking place in Zama City, Mackenzie County. Residents from that community were supposed to register at a reception centre in High Level. The existence of the two evacuation centres, combined with an initial lack of communication between Mackenzie County and Dene Tha' First Nation, caused confusion. Most Taché evacuees, including bus passengers, went to the High Level reception centre set up for Zama City. One Taché resident recalled that once they arrived at High

Level, it was "all over the place. Like, we had no information where we were supposed to go, who was a contact person. We went through town council, and they directed us to the place where there was agencies, and then I was all over the place. It was just completely out of it."

Multistage Evacuations by Air

Some First Nations in Canada are located in regions accessible only by air, boat, or winter roads. Often these communities are small, but some can be home to as many as four thousand people. The majority of these communities are located deep in the boreal forests of northern Saskatchewan, Manitoba, Ontario, and Quebec. Evacuating fly-in communities requires a massive coordinated effort by First Nations and multiple external government agencies, including the Department of National Defence, which sends aircraft if requested. As former evacuees of two fly-in communities – Deer Lake and Sandy Lake – recalled, communities and agencies can encounter multiple problems, including

- lack of transportation to the airport
- lack of preparation and fear of flying
- delays at airport hangars
- confusion about the ultimate destination
- separation of families.

> Evacuating fly-in communities requires a massive coordinated effort by First Nations and multiple external government agencies, including the Department of National Defence, which sends aircraft.

Deer Lake First Nation

Deer Lake, which evacuated nearly one thousand residents in July 2011, encountered all of these problems. At first, some people had no way to get to the airport, and when they did arrive, there was no structure to the boarding. One resident recalled: "They should have a more structured list of people. Like when they were going down to the last couple flights, they were just throwing random people on. Just because these people weren't at the airport. Or they should have gave them rides to the airport if they didn't have a ride. That's why people were missing flights." People who had a management role during the evacuation and other community members assisted by helping to load the planes.

Once they got on the planes, flying in large, noisy military cargo planes proved to be uncomfortable for some evacuees, particularly Elders, people who were ill, and other high-risk residents. The spouse of an Elder from Deer Lake First Nation explained:

> There was really sick people, and we were just in that Hercules. It was really hard for my husband, 'cause we were just sitting on the floor, and we were just really packed in that Hercules. At that time, my husband was already getting weak. They had seats for them, and I didn't tell that my husband needed a seat, and they just shoved us on the floor. And when the Hercules went, and he fell down, and I had to get him up. But anyways, it was pretty hard when we were sitting on the floor. My feet are sleeping, 'cause we had a whole bunch of us, and we didn't have room to move around, so we had to sit there until we got to Thunder Bay. That's over an hour ride like that. That was really hard.

During the first evacuation, on July 6, evacuees travelled to Geraldton, Ontario, where they stayed during the evacuation. During the second partial evacuation, on July 21, they flew to Thunder Bay, where they stayed in the airport hangar overnight. The next day, they continued to Toronto and then travelled by bus to the town of Smiths Falls, near Ottawa. One resident remembered: "My wife said there was cots and really thin blankets, but they left the hangar doors open, and you know how big hangar doors are. And they left the door open, and they said they got pretty cold that night."

While they waited at the hangar, some evacuees had no idea where they were being sent because they had not been given that information by Emergency Management Ontario or other personnel in charge of the evacuation. This caused frustration and some anger. One resident recalled:

> They took us to Thunder Bay first, and then from there we didn't even know where we were going. They told us, at first, Toronto. They told us we were going to Thunder Bay. And then from there, they were gonna tell us where we were gonna go. But when we got to Thunder Bay, they told us, "We're moving you, and we're going." And then there were just rumours ... At first they said Toronto, 'cause Geraldton was full. 'Cause they usually send us to Geraldton. And that summer there was a lot of fires, so Thunder Bay was full, so that's why they took us on to ... We landed in Toronto on a jet plane.

Once they arrived in Toronto, another evacuee recalled: "They just brought a bus up and said, 'We're leaving.' They didn't say anything; they didn't tell us anything. We didn't know where we were going, not until the bus driver told us we were going to Smiths Falls, when we asked him where that was, because we had no idea where that was."

Sandy Lake First Nation

Residents of Sandy Lake faced similar but different problems when they evacuated that same year. With no evacuation plan, the Chief relied on assistance from community nurses to quickly identify residents who were at high risk from smoke who would need to leave in a partial evacuation. As the Chief explained: "There was no set guideline at that time, and we weren't following a book saying 'Here's what you do in this case.' Basically, we just took charge right from the beginning, and it was common sense, things that we did, no-brainer things that tells here's a step, here's what we need to do next."

But some residents who were evacuated two days later as part of the full evacuation did not anticipate that they would have to leave

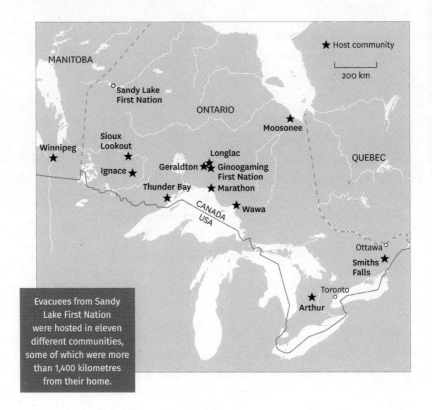

★ Host community

⊢————————⊣
200 km

MANITOBA

ONTARIO

QUEBEC

○ Sandy Lake
First Nation

Moosonee ★

Winnipeg
★

Sioux
Lookout
★

Longlac
Geraldton ★★ Ginoogaming
First Nation

Ignace ★

Thunder Bay
★

★ Marathon

CANADA
USA

★ Wawa

Ottawa ○

Smiths ★
Falls

Toronto
○

Arthur ★

Evacuees from Sandy Lake First Nation were hosted in eleven different communities, some of which were more than 1,400 kilometres from their home.

and were unprepared: "We didn't know. I had to run home and pack my bags, and I didn't even bring my phone charger and stuff like that. It was just like that – the 'last plane is going now,' 'you're going' kind of thing. So that's how I ended up going." Another evacuee explained the problem: "Well, at first we weren't sure if we were going to be the ones who evacuated, because all they said was for the priority, which are the babies and the chronically ill, that was what they said. As for the rest of us, we didn't think we were going to go, you know, be evacuated. So we weren't prepared at all."

Evacuees in the partial evacuation were sent to Sioux Lookout (450 kilometres away) and Thunder Bay (650 kilometres away), where they were hosted in hotel rooms. For the full community evacuation, residents stayed in nine communities, towns, or cities in Ontario: Arthur, Geraldton, Ginoogaming First Nation, Ignace,

Long-lac, Marathon, Moosonee, Smiths Falls, and Wawa. Some evac-uees were also sent to Winnipeg, Manitoba. Most travelled to the host communities via Thunder Bay, where they stayed for an average of twelve hours without knowing their ultimate destination. One evacuee recalled that they stayed at the hangar all day and that "it was in the evening, around 9 p.m., it was already getting dark by the time we were on the bus. We were not told while you were staying there. We were not given information where we were going or how long will we stay there." Another participant recalled people getting impatient and that waiting was particularly challenging for children.

A man whose wife and two of his children had been evacuated in the partial evacuation to Sioux Lookout recalled that he and his other two children had had to line up and wait for the buses. He only found out they were heading to the city of Marathon after he got on the bus:

> First of all, I got shipped to Thunder Bay. I guess that's where everybody got sent to, and from there everybody got dispensed out to various locations. And I didn't know where I was going. Nobody mentioned this is where you're going, this is the place everybody's going to go. It's more like you're sitting there, and all of a sudden, "Line up." We were told to line up, and I didn't know, and they didn't say where we were going ... I knew my wife was already in Sioux Lookout, and she didn't know where I was going. And, finally, I told her that this is where I am after I got situated, the next day.

Multistage Road Evacuations

As the examples of Sandy Lake and Deer Lake reveal, fly-in com-munities typically need to be evacuated in stages, which can pose multiple transportation problems. Evacuees need to be taken to one location, where they then wait, sometimes overnight, before moving on to a second location and sometimes even a third. However, multi-stage evacuations can also occur in First Nations communities with road access, as the evacuations of Stanley Mission in north-central Saskatchewan in 2014 (a full evacuation) and 2015 (a partial evacuation) illustrate. In this case, the community had road access, but it was a single gravel road, and blockades of nearby roads because of other fires complicated the evacuations. Evacuees had to travel to the larger cities of Saskatoon (in central Saskatchewan) and Regina (in southern Saskatchewan). As evacuees made their way through the province, either in their own vehicles or by bus, they made multiple stops and received guidance at each stage of the process.

The Pikangikum Evacuations, 2019

Pikangikum First Nation, an Ojibwe community home to over 3,000 residents, is one of the largest First Nations in northwestern Ontario. The community is accessible by winter road, but it is a fly-in community during warmer weather. During the summer of 2019, the community experienced two wildfire evacuation events.

On Wednesday, May 29, 2019, a wildfire grew rapidly near the community. It damaged the broadband communication line servicing the community and knocked out all phone and internet services. Despite the Chief's immediate requests for an evacuation, external agencies were slow to respond because of complications surrounding arranging for air evacuation in heavy smoke. An emailed statement from Ontario Indigenous Affairs said that it was unsure if the aircraft sent could land safely on the community airstrip, so a low-altitude inspection would have to be completed first. Chief Amanda Sainnawap described the scene as chaos as hundreds of high-risk residents waited to be evacuated. Evacuations began on Thursday evening, and sixteen hundred residents eventually relocated to communities in Ontario and Manitoba for a few weeks.

On July 6, 2019, another wildfire started near Pikangikum, resulting in a second evacuation by bus, boat, and aircraft. The community immediately began to evacuate their most vulnerable residents, but the next day instituted a full evacuation of all residents. On July 10, the evacuation was paused because there were no host communities. The Ontario government put out a plea to mayors across Ontario to host evacuees, and the First Nation began looking for host communities in Manitoba and Saskatchewan. A week after the evacuation was ordered, only half of the community had evacuated. On July 14, the evacuation was put on hold because the fire risk had decreased substantially. A few days later, evacuees began to return to the community.

The Full Evacuation, 2014

In 2014, when the first evacuation of Stanley Mission was called, essential staff organized check-in tables at the Band Hall. Each table contained lists, including a list of community members with chronic conditions. The band council hoped to organize and track who needed to leave the community, who remained, and who had left. Most evacuees recalled that the plan went quite well:

> There was no mass panic. There was people who were answering the telephones at the Band Hall, at the band office, and how well the different [local] agencies worked together. Now, I don't know what it's like in other communities, but in this community it actually works very well together. Because all the different [local] agencies all get together on a regular basis.

Staff prepared food, including sandwiches, to give to waiting evacuees and told evacuees with their own transportation to go to the band-owned Jonas Roberts Memorial Community Centre (JRMCC) hall in La Ronge, where they could register with the Red Cross. One resident recalled: "They inform the people that if they're gonna be takin' off in their own vehicles, to go to the gas bar and let the workers there know that they're on that evacuee list, evacuation list. Then they give you a certain amount of what to gas up, like thirty or forty bucks."

The majority of evacuees did not have their own transportation and waited at the Band Hall to board school buses, which would take them to La Ronge. They could only bring minimal things with them, such as a small bag. One mother complained that because she could not bring her child's car seat, she had to hold her small baby for the five-hour bus ride.

Organizers assigned people buses in a particular order. One resident recalled:

> Before everybody gets evacuated, there is an order. The chronics have to go first, and those are people who have respiratory problems, pregnant women, children under twelve or children under two, and the elderly. They are the priority first. As soon as they get those ones out, if they don't have vehicles, then they will be the first ones to be listed to go on buses. If they have their own private vehicles, then you are expected to leave if you're on the chronic list.

Although the evacuation plan laid out how and in what order people would leave the community, it couldn't have foreseen that road closures would prevent residents who were outside Stanley Mission from returning to see their families or pick up possessions. These residents were told to go directly to La Ronge, where they would be provided with accommodations and meal vouchers.

At the JRMCC hall in La Ronge, the Red Cross registered evacuees who arrived on buses or on their own. It fed evacuees as they waited to switch buses or offered them food vouchers. Evacuees recalled that the scene was disorganized and chaotic compared to the Band Hall in Stanley Mission. Most wanted to stay in La Ronge because it was close to home, but others boarded buses that took them to Prince Albert or Saskatoon. Those who had evacuated in their own vehicles and did not want to stay in evacuation centres had to find and pay for their own accommodation. Those who had arrived by bus but did not want to travel south phoned family members to arrange for accommodation, and some booked and paid for their own rooms in local hotels in La Ronge. Provided they could afford it, it was money well spent. A few participants mentioned that the hardest part of the evacuation was the cramped, hours-long bus trip to host communities. A few buses arrived in Saskatoon from La Ronge in the middle of the night.

The Transportation
Needs of Elders

A comprehensive evacuation plan should take the particular transportation needs of Elders into consideration. During the evacuation of Stanley Mission, for instance, the Elders' care centre required a coordinated effort to evacuate. Eight Elders resided there, and each Elder had special physical and mental ailments and needs. Several were confined to wheelchairs. When the evacuation order came out, staff received calls letting them know they would be expected to accompany the Elders. One organizer commented: "First we had to get all the workers. Well, when you work for health and when the Elders here get evacuated, you have to go. You can't say no ... So we had to phone around and get all the other workers." Once staff arrived, they packed up a small bag for each Elder, including medication. One participant recalled having a difficult time with one Elder who had severe dementia and was physically aggressive. Staff and Elders were loaded into a community van and a taxi, which took them to the JRMCC hall in La Ronge.

The Partial Evacuation, 2015

In 2015, when the Stanley Mission band council decided to initiate a partial evacuation because of wildfire smoke, around six hundred residents participated in a second multistage evacuation. This time, band members who needed to evacuate were either notified by staff at the clinic, they found out by watching Channel 13 or listening to the radio, or they saw the order on Facebook. The local radio announcer reported on the evacuation in both English and Cree and explained what people had to do, where they were supposed to go, and who they should phone for more information. Evacuees recalled that they had little time to prepare and brought very little with them. The limited notice frustrated some who felt it reflected a lack of foresight by band leaders.

Staff members, however, said they felt they had been prepared to handle the evacuation because of their experience the previous year. One person recalled:

In the first month, I think we evacuated about six hundred people and that included all the priority people: the Elders, the pre- and post-natals, the babies less than two, and anybody with chronic respiratory problems. The thing about that is that when you're evacuating the pre- and post-natals and the babies and whatnot, their families have to go with them as well. So it's not only them that has to go, there's usually about three or four family members that have to go with them. We had it fairly organized this year because this is the second year that we've had fires.

Evacuees were asked to go to the Band Hall, where nurses, armed with the "chronic" list, set up check-in stations for each category of evacuee. The evacuation went smoothly because staff members had spent over a year working on their priority and chronic lists.

For those travelling on school buses, staff and volunteers made bag lunches that included sandwiches, juice boxes, fruit, and cookies. Evacuees, numbered during registration, were called to board certain buses. Although the process was organized, one evacuee described it as "hurry up and wait": "They have to go to the Band Hall, register, wait there, sit there for hours to get onto the bus just to travel to the La Ronge, wait there another couple hours to be transported to Saskatoon." And staff had to deal with a number of unanticipated problems, revealing that even when things are going well, organizers and caregivers should never take things for granted:

- An evacuee who thought he was having a heart attack had to be evacuated on a bus to La Ronge because of road closures.
- A child under two had difficulty breathing, and his parents were later told his lungs had begun to collapse because of the smoke.
- Some family members refused to accompany Elders, so responsibility fell to staff.
- Parents with children slightly older than two became frustrated because they wanted to evacuate their children, but the band would not cover the costs.

- A community member with chronic health conditions in the hospital in La Ronge had to be evacuated farther south to Saskatoon.
- Some residents evacuated even though they were not in a high-risk group.

On the latter point, one resident remarked: "Lasting negative effect would be that there was people that left that shouldn't have left, that shed bad light on this emergency situation ... They live an unhealthy lifestyle, so they knew the things they needed would not be coming to the community, so they left for easier access ... They couldn't get their drugs and alcohol."

As during the 2014 evacuation, when the evacuees arrived at the JRMCC hall in La Ronge, they registered and eventually transferred to buses to take them farther south. An emergency response coordinator from La Ronge organized the evacuation, but evacuees often did not know which host community they were travelling to. And road closures affected the evacuation. Instead of travelling directly from Stanley Mission to La Ronge and then on to host communities such as Prince Albert, Saskatoon, and Regina, evacuees took multiple detours, which extended the length of the trip substantially: "We had to wait for sometimes two hours before we could pass there. They took it to a different direction. We went east and from there to Prince Albert. We didn't go all the way from La Ronge to Prince Albert because they blocked those roads because there was fires down there. That's why they did it." Evacuees who were sent to Regina arrived at the evacuation centre just after 5 a.m. the next morning, after spending five to seven hours on a bus. Participants noted that a few evacuees with babies were not allowed to bring car seats and had to hold their babies during the entire trip.

As these examples show, the actual evacuation from a community is seldom straightforward, and many issues can arise when moving multiple people from their homes, particularly in a stressful situation. By looking at past evacuations, we can learn from what went well and what went wrong, improving our awareness to better anticipate potential issues and respond to future evacuations.

Guiding Questions for First Nations

- Do you know the recommended evacuation routes? Do you know which host community (or communities) evacuees are going to? Do you have a plan to communicate that information to members?
- Do you have a plan for assisting residents who do not have their own transportation out of the community?
- Do you have a list of Elders with special transportation needs? Do you know where they reside, who their closest relatives are, and who will care for them?
- Is there a plan for reimbursing local gas stations to ensure that those residents with private vehicles will have enough gas to make it to a safe location? Will you provide gas money or mileage for band members? How will you keep track of these expenses?
- For long evacuations, do you have a plan to feed evacuees before they leave the community or provide them with food and water for their trip?

Guiding Questions for External Agencies

- How will you assist First Nations to ensure that the evacuees can leave their community?
- Has it been made clear which expenses will be reimbursed (e.g., mileage, food, and so on)?
- Are you effectively communicating to the evacuees about where they are expected to go and how they should get there?
- For communities that may require air evacuation, have the facilities in the First Nation been assessed recently? What size plane can land on the runway? How long would it take to evacuate the community by air? How many aircraft would be needed?

Community Spotlight

Deer Lake First Nation, Ontario

Deer Lake First Nation is a small fly-in community of 1,100 people located near the Manitoba border, north of Red Lake and 700 kilometres northwest of Thunder Bay. The community is located in northern Ontario's Canadian Shield and is surrounded by fire-prone boreal forests and a labyrinth of lakes. People in Deer Lake speak Oji-Cree, a blend of Anishinaabemowin and Cree. The Nation has a school (K–9), health centre, daycare centre, churches, a baseball field, a hockey rink, a nursing station, and a northern store. A white "Hollywood" sign high on a hill outside the settlement was built by community members.

On July 6, 2011, wildfires burning close to the local airport, combined with smoke that impacted air quality, led to the partial evacuation of about 500 residents. They were flown out in Canadian Forces Hercules aircraft and returned home seven days later. On July 21, a second partial evacuation of 550 residents was called as wildfires again came close to the community. These residents were evacuated by Hercules aircraft for two weeks.

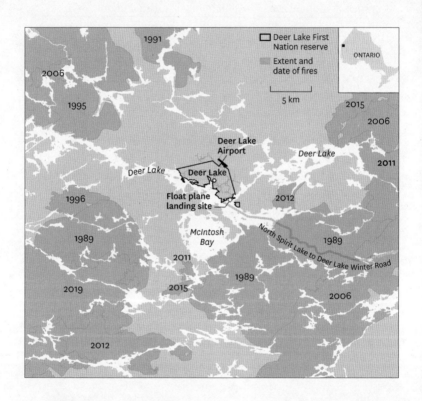

Deer Lake is a fly-in-only community. When a wildfire threatened the First Nation, residents were evacuated by a Canadian Forces Hercules transport aircraft.

4.

FINDING ACCOMMODATIONS

There was a team that met us there and they fed us right away. They took us off the bus, and they fed us, and they gave us juice and got us going. They put us up in hotels.

— RESIDENT, MISHKEEGOGAMANG OJIBWAY NATION

ONCE EVACUEES HAVE gone through the long and stressful process of leaving their homes and communities by plane, car, or bus, they want to rest and recuperate in a place where they feel comfortable while they wait to return home. Accommodation for evacuees is organized by the host community and may include hotels, evacuation centres, or other temporary places that have facilities suitable for housing people such as school rooms and gymnasiums or recreation and community centres. The options can vary from province to province or from community to community. For example, evacuation centres are less commonly used in Alberta, where the preference is to have people stay in hotel rooms. In Saskatchewan, agreements between Indigenous Services Canada, the provincial government, and the Red Cross mean that most evacuees stay in centres run by the Red Cross. Evacuees from Ontario, by contrast, stay in a mix of hotel rooms and evacuation centres.

As our discussion on troubleshooting transportation emphasizes, evacuation organizers should have processes in place to let community members know well in advance who their host community is and where they should go once they arrive at the destination. The problems encountered by First Nations at this stage of an evacuation will also help community leaders and host communities understand the costs and benefits of choosing one form of accommodation over another (for example, hotels versus evacuation centres) and how to avoid setting up communities in inappropriate accommodations. On this latter point, during the 2011 evacuation of Deer Lake First Nation, some evacuees were flown out of their remote northwestern Ontario community and accommodated in the Rideau Regional Centre, which evacuees later referred to as the "sanatorium." The centre had been closed down two years earlier, and the problems associated with its use stand as yet another warning about the dangers of agencies and host communities not having a well-coordinated evacuation plan. Organizers also need to plan for residents seeking alternative accommodations in host communities.

> Accommodation for evacuees is organized
> by the host community.

The Pros and Cons of Hotels

Compared with evacuation centres, hotels hold many benefits for First Nations communities, but they also have limitations that community leaders and host communities should take into consideration when putting together an evacuation plan. For First Nations communities leery of institutional settings that can trigger memories of residential schools, hotels offer privacy and a setting where families can live together and share and prepare food. An evacuee from Stanley Mission recalled that "the room we stayed in had a microwave and a little fridge, so we kinda, like, shared our foods. We bought TV dinners or noodles that you can microwave in a bowl for the kids. Then we kinda split [the cost of groceries]."

When family and community members stay in the same hotel, they can support one another and share resources during an evacuation. An evacuee from Mishkeegogamang Ojibway Nation recalled: "Having money kinda made it easier. Like with some of the families that didn't have it, they struggled, and some of their kids would be, like, 'I'm hungry,' and all that kinda stuff. So being with my family and them supporting me and just helping each other out, that helped

Recreation centres, like this one in High Prairie, Alberta, often become reception centres for evacuees.
Photo: Tara McGee

a lot." Some First Nations reported that they also had staff who worked or volunteered as security at the hotels. These staff members played a difficult but vital role, providing information and a sense of safety for evacuees in need.

Although hotels offered these benefits, overcrowding can be a problem, particularly when host communities are serving multiple First Nations during wide-ranging wildfires. During Whitefish Lake First Nation's evacuation to High Prairie, for example, some large families spread out into several rooms, but each room was crowded with six or seven people for weeks at a time. Likewise, an evacuee from the Dene Tha' community of Taché recalled that when they took up their hotel room in High Level, it had a single room, two beds and no cot, for six people. An Elder from Sandy Lake First Nation concurred: "We were crowded too much. Like in that one room there was my sister and my brother-in-law and then another one of my sister's granddaughters was there and also myself. That's five in two beds that were double beds. And if you needed to get some rest you couldn't. Too crowded."

As one would expect, in some cases tensions rose, and the stress of overcrowding in hotels was heightened by the fact that, unlike in evacuation centres, in some cases there were no activities planned for children and youth. In some cases, parties were held in hotel rooms, upsetting evacuees and hotel staff. An evacuee from Whitefish Lake recalled that the "youth were hard to keep in High Prairie 'cause ... so much energy that they have to burn. And us mostly, we just stayed at the room and tried to get them to do stuff ... Yeah, they were getting bored. They wanted to go home." An evacuee from Sandy Lake explained that being cooped up inside can be particularly difficult for First Nations people:

Many of the people here, not everybody leaves the reserve. So, again, there's the difference in culture; living on reserve versus living off the reserve, especially the young children ... We're talking outside right now. You notice how calm it is, how free it is, right? You take that away from us and put us in hotel rooms. You put us where we cannot walk around, right? And to learn how to adapt and change our lifestyles all of a sudden is very hard.

A community liaison from Mishkeegogamang agreed: "It was pretty hard for the families to be staying in the room, 'cause you always have to watch, make sure you don't break anything, or nobody gets hurt. It was like as if we were cooped up."

Even though a host community may have a plan to house evacuees in hotels, there is no guarantee that rooms will be available. Evacuees from both Whitefish Lake and Taché had difficulty finding hotel rooms. As mentioned, when evacuees from Whitefish Lake arrived in High Prairie, they went to the local Gordon Buchanan Recreation Centre to register for hotel accommodations. But they learned that local hotels had no vacancies because residents of Gift Lake Métis Settlement had evacuated to the same host community. While some Whitefish Lake evacuees kept driving on to Valleyview or Grande Prairie, one couple ended up sleeping in their car for the first night of the evacuation, then drove to stay with friends the next day. Several evacuees from Taché stayed in a motel for a few days but were then told that their rooms were no longer available. Motel staff and evacuation organizers informed them that they would have to find another motel because the rooms had been reserved by government employees. This was an inconvenience for the evacuees, who then had to move to a motel across the street.

These examples highlight the problems that can arise when an evacuation plan is dependent on hotels. Host communities should ask:

- Is there a back-up plan if hotels quickly fill up?
- Is there a priority system to ensure that high-risk residents and residents with special needs get rooms?

Prioritizing Elders

Staff and organizers should ensure that Elders have private, comfortable accommodation during an evacuation not only because of the role, recognition, and respect Elders possess within their communities but also because of the physical challenges many of them experience such as limited mobility or chronic health conditions. During the evacuation of Whitefish Lake, Mishkeegogamang, Taché, and Sandy Lake, Elders were given first priority for hotel rooms. During Taché's evacuation, many Elders had to wait in the school gym overnight, but others went to a motel room right away. By contrast, when First Nations evacuated to host communities without organized hotel accommodation, they had to stay in evacuation centres. Elders from Stanley Mission, for example, were treated like everyone else until band staff complained that the cots in the evacuation centre were too high for Elders to get in and out of.

It is also vital that Elders receive information. Many Elders speak only their traditional language, so translators are needed to help them understand announcements. Translator roles are often filled unofficially by family members, but the First Nation should ensure that there are translators available at evacuation centres or hotels where Elders are staying.

The Pros and Cons of Evacuation Centres

In many host communities, evacuees are housed in large evacuation centres, usually converted hockey arenas or sports centres. These large open spaces typically include cots arranged to maximize the number of people who can stay in the space. But the benefits of housing large numbers of people must be weighed against the limitations – lack of privacy and the negative associations that institutional settings have for many First Nations people.

But evacuation centres can be a positive experience. When Mishkeegogamang was evacuated in summer 2011, only a few dozen evacuees, mainly adults, were sent to Geraldton, Ontario. The small number of evacuees meant that they had room in the evacuation centre to spread out, which created more of a camping atmosphere. One resident recalled: "We all stayed in what looked like an arena, indoor rink. The rink was pretty big, then there was a whole bunch of beds in there that we had to choose from ... It was the rec centre, I think. It was nice though."

In contrast, when hundreds of evacuees stay together in evacuation centres, the atmosphere can be quite different. An evacuee sent from Mishkeegogamang to Sioux Lookout recalled that community members stayed in a crowded arena full of "kids screaming and stuff" before being moved into a hotel. Another recalled that "it was too hard for the pregnant women to sleep on the hard floor, and there was no privacy. So we asked if at least they could give hotel rooms to the pregnant women and the Elders." An evacuee from Sandy Lake remembered that when her parents stayed in Geraldton "they did not like it because there is no privacy. Our Elders like privacy. They should have partitions for the Elders. They even had classrooms. They should have put the Elders there."

Understandably, evacuees who stay in evacuation centres find it difficult to sleep with so many other people close by, children making noise during the night, and, in some cases, security lights shining down on them. Sleeping on cots was challenging not only for pregnant women but also for some Elders. An Elder from Lac La Ronge Indian Band who participated in the evacuation of Stanley Mission

Evacuation centres in places like hockey arenas can be uncomfortable to stay in due to noise, crowding, a lack of privacy, and intrusive surveillance.
Photo: Jeff Putnam/CP

in 2014 mentioned that it was a long walk to the bathroom facilities, and a few other evacuees mentioned that their children were cold at night because of the air conditioning. Communal bathroom facilities also reduced privacy.

> Some evacuees likened the experience of staying in an evacuation centre to prison.

During Lac La Ronge's 2015 evacuation, when wildfires raged throughout Saskatchewan, evacuation centres in Saskatoon and Regina had to take in evacuees from different First Nations communities. Overcrowding forced some mothers to share narrow green cots with their babies. Fights broke out between evacuees. One community member thought the second evacuation was worse "because there were lots of people from all over, from different reserves. They put us all together ... Those people got in trouble; they got locked up; some of them fought in the middle of the night."

Evacuees likened the experience of staying in an evacuation centre to prison. They said that the Red Cross asking them to sign in and out when they left or returned made them feel as if they were in jail:

> A lot of people said that when they were taken out over there, it was like being in prison. They weren't free to come and go as they wanted ... There was too many rules. This year [2015], a lot of people didn't really wanna go ... The ones that had healthy children, they chose not to go because they said it was like being in a prison when they were over there. So that's one thing that didn't work.

Others recalled that there were so many Red Cross staff and security guards that they felt uncomfortable: "It was like you were under constant watch. I don't think that was needed ... It's like when you go, when you're a Native person and you go shopping at Walmart. There's always somebody looking."

The Evacuation of Deer Lake First Nation

During the first evacuation of Deer Lake on June 6, 2011, evacuees were flown to Geraldton, Ontario. They stayed in the arena, where they experienced typical issues such as lack of privacy and problems sleeping. During the partial evacuation of July 21, however – when evacuees were flown to Smiths Falls, near the national capital, and hosted at the Rideau Regional Centre – they were placed in an environment that was entirely inappropriate. Built for people with developmental disabilities in 1963, the centre had closed in 2009. One evacuee recalled that "it looked like a hospital, but it was for psychiatric care and stuff like that." Another explained that it was a last resort: "It was an abandoned building, and they weren't using it for anything. But it was a big place, and they were looking for a big place to put all these evacuees, and I think practically everybody was evacuated, even Sandy Lake and all those other people, and there was no other place."

Evacuees from Deer Lake First Nation felt haunted during their stay at the Rideau Regional Centre, a former institution for people with developmental disabilities.
Photo: Marc Perreault

Most of the evacuees slept on cots in rooms or hallways, but some evacuees, mostly children, slept on the floor because they were not given a cot. One evacuee recalled: "I was supposed to be in the hallway and the rooms, and they kept blocking, so people are getting stuck in the room or couldn't get into their room. And there was only one master key for how many rooms." Although organizers did the best they could to clean the centre up, evacuees recalled that some rooms smelled, and the shower stalls in the common washrooms had no curtains or doors.

Many evacuees said everyone was frightened by the centre, by eerie noises and sightings of "people in white clothing, like doctors, like hospital clothes, or shapes of humans." One evacuee recounted a few stories:

> One time, we were outside, and upstairs we seen the light go on and the light went off, and we went to check it out. There's nobody up there. And there was this lady that had groceries on the floor, and she had just put it on the floor, and then they were getting ready to sleep, and all of a sudden somebody was digging around. They turned the lights on. Nobody was there. That's what they were saying.

And then there was this other one. She said somebody touched her on her leg, like, she felt a hand.

And those boys. They stole the master key, and they said, "We seen a little girl running down the hall." And they were going after that little girl, and when they thought they were almost getting to her, she disappeared. And then again they seen her going down the hall again. They ran after her, and they said they were running after a little girl.

But I heard lots of stuff. Even one of the kids had his ... you know those games that – I forgot what it's called – anyways, it takes pictures, and he said that his game was closed. When he put it down, it was open, and there's a picture of a person on the window. That's what he was sayin', and he got scared because his parents were securities at night, and they stayed in that room, and he didn't wanna stay in that room by himself 'cause of what he had seen.

Another resident said his son and my daughter had nightmares when they got home and that he would never go back there ever again.

Spirituality varies from First Nation to First Nation, but most Indigenous Peoples in Canada feel a close connection to the spirit world. Indigenous Peoples grow up surrounded by stories of otherworldly beings. For these evacuees, the sanatorium was not simply a derelict building with physical problems; it housed negative energy that emanated from the experiences of former occupants. Their experiences in the evacuation centre had a lasting negative effect, particularly on children.

Alternative Accommodations

Evacuees from fly-in communities and those who take the bus typically stay in evacuation centres or hotels. But evacuees with their own vehicles can opt out and seek alternative accommodations, although they are often still required to register at the evacuation centre to receive financial aid. For example, one couple from Whitefish Lake slept in their car on the first night of the evacuation and then drove to stay with friends. An evacuee from Mishkeegogamang who was in Thunder Bay at the time of the evacuation stayed with family living in the city. Some evacuees from Taché stayed with friends and family either in High Level or Bushe River. Most evacuees from Stanley Mission who left in their own vehicle stayed with family or friends in La Ronge, Prince Albert, or other smaller Indigenous communities in the area.

A caregiver who was looking after evacuees from Whitefish Lake explained that Elders would have been more comfortable camping out in the bush than in a hotel. A community leader from Mishkeegogamang also suggested that a camp environment would have been more comfortable for evacuees and community leaders who had to take care of evacuees in hotels:

> I think I'd rather be in a camp area, camp setting, instead of a town in a hotel room ... I think that would be really good. 'Cause we're used to ... In the community, everybody knows each other, and everybody does things together – instead of [community leaders] being afraid for your people when you go in a city or a town. Gives you some kind of relief, I guess ... As long as we have a vehicle just in case somebody gets sick.

A few evacuees from Stanley Mission said they would rather have stayed with another First Nation such as the Rez Cross set up at Beardy's and Okemasis First Nation (see next page). The Red Cross, however, would only support evacuees in its own centres:

> And there was also other reserves that did open up their reserves, [but] they had to get approved by Red Cross to be an official evacuee centre. And they had smoke houses and shades outside, and you saw pictures of these people that were outside enjoying the sun under these shades. And there was even a guy from Hall Lake that was smoking deer meat that somebody had donated, and they were talking about traditional food. As I was stuck with Subway,

McDonald's, Burger King, Pizza Hut ... they were having dry meat, and they were having bannock, and they were having fun.

The Rez Cross

During the July 2015 wildfires in Saskatchewan, Beardy's and Okemasis First Nation in Treaty 6 territory north of the city of Saskatoon set up their own evacuation centre at their hockey arena. Called the Rez Cross, the centre was certified by the Prince Albert Grand Council to function as an official evacuation centre. On July 8, Councillor Kevin Seesquasis reported to the CBC that sixty-three evacuees from Lac La Ronge Indian Band communities (including Hall Lake, La Ronge, and Grandmother's Bay) were staying at the Rez Cross. The centre, however, had room for three hundred. The band advertised its evacuation centre via social media. Evacuees staying at the Rez Cross could participate in activities such as horseback riding and hunting and cultural events such as powwows. The First Nation accepted donations from across the province.

Beardy's and Okemasis Cree Nation's hockey arena became an evacuation centre known as the Rez Cross. Evacuees were treated like guests and invited to participate in activities like horseback riding, hunting, and powwows.
Photo: Victoria Dinh/CBC

Although alternative arrangements can give evacuees more control, problems can still occur. For example, one evacuee from Whitefish Lake stayed with twenty-four people in a two-bedroom apartment: "We were like sardines in the house, but I didn't wanna go. I can't stand hotels." Another stayed with three families in a holiday trailer: "I told them I was in a trailer, and I was going to go stay at the campsite. There was me, my husband, my son, just the three of us, but then my daughter and her kids. There were twelve of us in my trailer." This may be manageable for a few days but the evacuation lasted three weeks.

Regardless of where evacuees end up – hotel, private home, or a centre run by the community – host communities should do everything within their power to ensure that accommodations are livable and culturally appropriate.

Guiding Questions for First Nations
- Which communities could you evacuate to, if needed? Have you met with these potential host communities to discuss accommodations that would be available for community members?
- Do you have appropriate accommodations available, if you are asked to host evacuees?
- Will you use band staff or volunteers to provide security at the evacuation centre or hotels?
- Will you have advocates or community liaisons who can ensure that evacuees' needs are being met?

Guiding Questions for External Agencies
- Do you have a list of host communities that can host evacuees if needed?
- Do all potential host communities have enough space and appropriate accommodations?
- How will you let the First Nation know which host communities are available? How will you decide which one(s) to use? Will the First Nation have a say?

Guiding Questions for Host Communities

- Do you have appropriate accommodation available?
- If hotel rooms are used for accommodation during an evacuation, will there be enough rooms and beds?
- Can evacuees be accommodated in rooms such as schoolrooms or offices, which can provide them with some privacy?
- Can Elders, pregnant women, and young children be prioritized for hotels or other private rooms?
- Can curtains be used in evacuation centres (if needed) to give evacuees some privacy?

Community Spotlight

Mishkeegogamang Ojibway Nation, Ontario

Mishkeegogamang Ojibway Nation is located on the Canadian Shield and in the boreal forests of northwestern Ontario. It has a population of about 1,900 people, and around 1,000 people live on reserve. The reserve is divided into two parts: reserve 63A, on the south shore of Lake St. Joseph, and reserve 63B, to the north of the lake, surrounding Dog Hole Bay. The Nation is accessible year-round by Highway 599, which starts in the town of Ignace and ends thirty-three kilometres to the north in the small community of Pickle Lake, which contains the local airport and the nearest store. Sioux Lookout, 230 kilometres to the southwest, provides health services, grocery stores, and other stores and services.

Community services in Mishkeegogamang include a health centre, family assistance, churches, police, a radio station, a K–8 school, and a community centre. A lodge that hosts community activities is located on Pashkokogan Lake. Hunting, trapping, fishing, and berry picking are important activities and sources of food to supplement store-bought provisions.

The summer of 2011 was one of the worst years for wildfires in northern Ontario – 1,330 wildfires burned 632,533 hectares. One of the two largest fires, the Sioux Lookout Fire 35, grew to 112,000 hectares and caused the evacuation of Mishkeegogamang Ojibway Nation in June. The evacuation was carried out over three days so that those at highest risk could leave first. Fortunately, no lives or structures were lost because of the fire. After ten days, evacuees returned home.

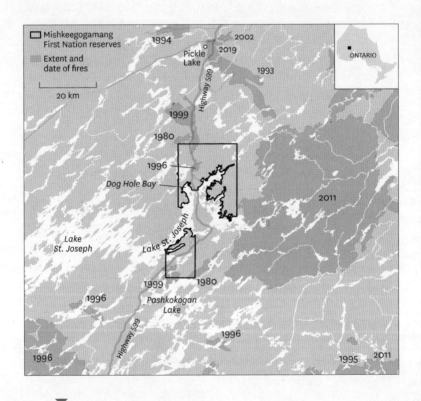

A large wildfire led to the evacuation
of the Mishkeegogamang Ojibway
Nation in 2011.

5.

TAKING CARE OF EVACUEES

We didn't do much really. They'd have activities at the gymnasium, or whatever, but I never really went to check it out. It's good to know at least they had something to keep us busy while we were over there.
— RESIDENT, MISHKEEGOGAMANG OJIBWAY NATION

IN ADDITION TO providing a safe place to stay, a well-developed evacuation plan should ensure that evacuees have access to nourishing and comforting food, activities to keep them busy during the day, up-to-date information, and special caretaking measures for evacuees with health conditions. By sharing their experiences living in host communities, former evacuees provide answers to four key questions:

1 What type of food should be provided to evacuees?
2 What type of activities will they enjoy?
3 What is the best way to let people know about the safety of their communities and family members?
4 What special measures need to be taken to ensure that people with health conditions have the care they need and that people have what they need to survive from day to day?

They also reveal some logistical issues associated with trying to provide these services to large numbers of people and First Nations communities.

Food

In host communities, decisions need to be made about not only what type of food to serve but also where to serve it and how often. Organizers should consider the following questions:

1 Will meals be served communally in the evacuation centre, hotel, or another community restaurant, or will evacuees be provided with meal tickets for selected restaurants? In the case of the former, who will prepare the meals? In the case of the latter, will transportation be offered to off-site locations?

2 Will snacks be provided outside of designated meal times, or will evacuees be responsible for purchasing their own food and drink for snacks? Will they be reimbursed? Will direct financial support be given to those in financial difficulty?

Organizers should keep in mind that food is an important part of Indigenous cultures across Canada. Many First Nations people, including Elders, rely on traditional meat, berries, and other plants for part of their diet. During an evacuation, host communities often serve food that might be very different from what First Nations eat at home. In general, evacuees said they appreciated the food they received. However, some evacuees said they missed traditional foods such as wild meat and bannock. To alleviate homesickness and make people feel more comfortable, host communities can attempt to incorporate Indigenous foods into their menus. They can also invite other First Nations to participate. During the evacuation of Whitefish Lake First Nation, for example, nearby Sucker Creek First Nation prepared a few dinners of traditional food for evacuees.

> During the evacuation of Whitefish Lake First Nation, nearby Sucker Creek First Nation prepared a few dinners of traditional food for evacuees.

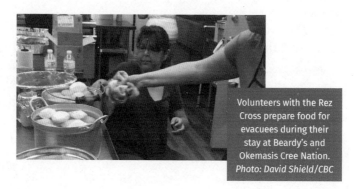

Volunteers with the Rez Cross prepare food for evacuees during their stay at Beardy's and Okemasis Cree Nation.
Photo: David Shield/CBC

Financial Support for Evacuees

Community leaders and evacuation planners must take the financial needs of First Nation evacuees into consideration. Evacuees may not have savings to carry them through the evacuation. Some may not have credit or debit cards, particularly Elders who may not have a bank account. In addition to providing money for gas so evacuees can leave the community, bands should also provide direct funds so evacuees can pay for essentials such as food and clothing. During the 2011 wildfire evacuations, the Government of Alberta provided adults with $1,250 and children with $500 for all evacuees in the province, including First Nations. However, this money was not distributed until weeks into the evacuations.

First Nations should ensure that this money is spent on items essential for the evacuation. Government agencies or the Red Cross may offer band members vouchers for local restaurants and purchase orders for groceries and gas. Not providing evacuees with adequate funding can be a real burden, particularly in northern communities where food is expensive. If bands are going to give money to evacuees (e.g., a councillor giving cash to an evacuee to cover diapers), there needs to be a plan to keep track of these expenses so they can be reimbursed when the evacuation is over.

Local residents helping to prepare and serve meals is also particularly enjoyed and appreciated by evacuees. A resident of Mishkeegogamang Ojibway First Nation recalled: "The people with Sioux Lookout, they were really good. They accepted us, and they ran a kitchen for us where there was a cook. They volunteered to cook with us, with some of our people. It was good. Even the young people helped, you know, teenagers helped. It was good to see." Evacuees also fondly recalled barbecues hosted by town mayors in Ontario.

Evacuees from Onion Lake First Nation who stayed at Harlan Hall were fed and received support from the Mennonite community. A participant commented that the experience made them closer to their non-Indigenous neighbours: "We had meals by the ladies. We know them now. It was a good meeting place for all of us to meet a ... and, yeah, we got fed well. And we got to visit each other because it made us closer because we were all terrified."

Although most former evacuees generally enjoyed meals and mealtime, some challenges arose, including

- meals being served at unfamiliar times and on tight schedules
- being subjected to racism in restaurants
- not having enough money to pay for meals.

Evacuees from both Stanley Mission and Whitefish Lake, who ate meals at evacuation centres, recalled that there were long lineups for meals, a particular concern for Elders: "Too many people, too crowded, a lot of lines to wait in." Others recalled that meals were served at odd times and on unfamiliar schedules. Some evacuees from Whitefish Lake explained that the designated breakfast time was too early, and some evacuees from Stanley Mission said they often felt rushed during meals.

They also remembered situations where someone in a restaurant made racist comments. For example, a community-liaison person from Stanley Mission who took Elders to a local restaurant for meals explained:

We had to take the Elders to the restaurant. That's one really bad problem we had, too, 'cause one of my workers had told me, "There's this one couple, white people, I guess they were complaining about the Elders there." Well, I wasn't there at that time, but they told me that this guy here was complaining about the Elders, saying that, "Why do you guys always have to bring your Elders here? Every time I come here to eat, this place is always full of your Elders. They're taking up all the room." "Why don't you take them someplace else, like [Prince Albert] or Saskatoon?" that guy said. My coworker told him, "Well, this is the place where they were sent, and they have to come, and they have to eat too," she said. And then she told him to mind his own business.

A similar incident occurred during the evacuation of Mishkee-gogamang.

Evacuees who stayed in other places had to arrange and in some cases pay for their own meals. Evacuees from Mishkeegogamang, for example, paid for their own food but were reimbursed by the band. In urgent circumstances, arrangements had to be made to send money to these evacuees during the evacuation. During the evacuation in 2015, the Red Cross gave evacuees from Stanley Mission who were staying with family or friends eighty-dollar vouchers for a week of food. One resident recalled:

They give me a voucher the first day, eighty dollars, and I asked that lady, "Just for a couple days?" and she said, "No, it's for a week." And I was trying to bug the lady, and I said, "Are you trying to put me on a diet?" There wasn't even a smile on her face. And I mean, it's kinda hard to go to a stranger's place, and then if you wanna get, and I mean eighty dollars ... It's not a whole lot.

Activities

In addition to providing meals, arrangements should also be made to plan activities to keep both adults and children occupied as evacuations of remote First Nations can often last for weeks. Swimming and other sports activities are easy to organize and enjoy. A resident from Mishkeegogamang recalled: "You'd go to sleep a while, and you wake up and start playing again, soccer or baseball. Stuff like that. We went to the beach. They took us around too. They had two buses they would take us about five, six miles out of Geraldton. There was a big nice beach there, but the water was cold [*laughs*]!" Evacuees also attended a couple of barbecues at the mayor's house.

During the evacuation of Stanley Mission in 2014, organizers arranged an activity for each day, including going to the zoo, movies, the mall, and swimming. A few parents noted that their children enjoyed the evacuation experience because of all the different activities they got to do; one mentioned it was like a vacation for the children. During the evacuation the following year, evacuees who stayed in Regina and Saskatoon likewise participated in various activities around the cities, including football games, swimming, shopping, visiting laundromats, and going to the park or a library. One participant spoke about the amazing work of the Gathering Place, run by Regina Treaty/Status Indian Services to assist First Nations transitioning between reserve and the city. Women cooked Indian tacos, neck bones, and bannock for evacuees. They also had bingo and set up other activities. Evacuees could also pick up donated items there, such as toiletries and clothing.

Youth particularly enjoy organized activities. A resident from Mishkeegogamang recalled that "there was these horses, and they took us out on a big wagon. I don't know what they are, like a horse ride and stuff like that. And they provided movie nights and different kinds of activities for our kids and families." Youth from Whitefish enjoyed these activities because they were not available on the reserve and provided an opportunity to take their minds off the wildfire and evacuation. One recalled:

> I just liked the sunny days and walking around, 'cause every time, when you walk around the street, you'd see a familiar face and just say hi and go have some company ... I didn't wanna keep the thing in the back of my mind, thinking the place was going to burn down, so I kept myself busy not thinking about it.

Potential Activities

There are countless activities that can be arranged at little expense, either at hotels, community centres, public parks, or private homes. These activities can be organized by host communities, external agencies, First Nations or individual band members, Indigenous organizations, or neighbouring Indigenous communities. Examples include

- cultural activities (ceremonies, powwows, traditional games)
- swimming at a hotel pool or nearby beach
- team sports and games such as baseball, football, or soccer
- barbecues
- visiting local sites such as zoos, malls, parks, or libraries
- seeing a movie
- movie and gaming nights for youths
- bingo and games nights.

As mentioned above, in some host communities, evacuees participated in arranged activities such as bingo that were similar to what would have taken place in their home community. Evacuees from Sandy Lake who were hosted in Ginoogaming First Nation enjoyed a barbecue, bingo, and a visit to cultural ceremony sites for events such as a powwow. One of the participants expressed her satisfaction with the activities provided during her stay:

The people were really nice over there. They even had a barbeque for us too. They showed us where they have their powwow in their community. They put three nights of bingo on for us. They asked us if we ever have rummage sales here, and we said yeah. They took us there. They had drivers to take us into town to go visit the other people from the community 'cause there was other ones [evacuees] over there inside the town [in nearby Longlac]. They tried to make us as comfortable as they could.

Although evacuees enjoy activities, some host communities in the past haven't provided them. An evacuee from Sandy Lake who stayed in Thunder Bay explained:

> Like all my sisters and my brother-in-law, we love to play bingo, but we didn't even get to go. I mean, what can we do for entertainment except stay in the hotel and watch TV? But you can't just watch TV all the time. I don't think I ever saw a movie that time. So there was really nothing except to go to the store. I don't think we ever really went anywhere except close by because of, like, why they couldn't arrange those [recreational activities]? Mount McKay and Chippewa Park, they have those. I think they still have those, right? We would have a better time if we were able to see more of the city, at least somewhere else anyway.

Some evacuees staying in host communities and elsewhere have organized their own activities or found other ways to keep themselves occupied. People visited local parks and libraries, picked out free clothing from a local thrift store, and spent time visiting other community members. Some evacuees went to meetings or looked at the information provided about the fire. But some had difficulty finding things to do that were affordable, particularly for children. An evacuee from Sandy Lake recalled: "If you ... actually look at the people that are walking around inside the lobbies, you know, it is very frustrating when you're out there with nothing. Some kids want to go to this place, but they can't because their parents can't afford to go there."

Often, those who do not participate in activities stay in their hotel room or other accommodation. An evacuee who looked after Elders in Mishkeegogamang said that most Elders stayed in their room during the evacuation except when they had meals. Evacuees from Whitefish Lake described the days as long and boring. Those not involved in providing security services spent days in their hotel rooms watching TV because they did not have additional spending money. When evacuees did leave their room, it was generally to go to the arena to visit with other evacuees and find out information about

Host communities often set up donation centres where evacuees can pick up clothing and other important items.
Photo: Jeff McIntosh/CP

the fire. Participants who evacuated to High Prairie and Grande Prairie recalled that many community members just wanted to eat and go back to their rooms because they were busy thinking about what was going on back home.

In some cases, if the host community is close to the wildfires, evacuees have no choice but to stay in. Low air quality because of wildfire smoke in High Level caused many evacuees from Dene Tha' First Nation's Taché community to spend most of their time in their hotel rooms to avoid the smoke. Evacuees were also not sure what else they could do. Staying in their rooms was difficult, particularly for children and youth used to spending a lot of time outdoors. One parent recalled:

My kids were stressed. They had no place to play around ... And then the kids are running around outside in the parking [lot] because they needed to tire themselves out. To go to the park with them, it was not good for me because I had asthma. The smoke was thick, and I was going through a lot of stress, and I just wanted to go home.

Knowledge Sharing

As the recollections of some evacuees reveal, evacuees want and need to receive accurate and timely information about the safety of their communities, homes, and families when they are living in a host community. Organizers should try to reach communities through as many routes as possible.

> Evacuees want and need to receive accurate and timely information about the safety of their communities, homes, and families when they are living in a host community.

Organizers should not rely on traditional news media to share knowledge about the safety of the First Nation communities. During the wildfire evacuation of Whitefish Lake, for example, most news media coverage in Alberta focused on the town of Slave Lake, which lost more than 340 houses and community infrastructure in a different fire. One resident recalled how these reports made his community feel: "We listened to the radio. All they ever did was talk about Gift Lake and Slave Lake. How 'bout us? The white guy put us on this reserve here, and they should be looking after us here too. We are just a little dot here on this reserve."

Organizers can provide information about the location of the wildfire and its impact on the community in various ways, but in general the process follows two stages: (1) information gathering in home communities and (2) information sharing in host communities.

Information Gathering in Home Communities

Community leaders typically engage in daily briefing sessions with government agencies and community liaisons in host communities. A community liaison for Stanley Mission's evacuation in 2015 explained:

I spent a lot of time over at the band office attending these meetings. Chief Tammy Cook-Searson would chair the meetings every morning. We'd find out exactly where the fires were, whether they were contained, whether they were wildfires, how close they were to our community or other communities, and whether we were in danger or not. We would also do a little report every day to tell them how the smoke was in the community. They would also inform us which roads were open, which roads were closed, and what the weather was gonna be doing and what we were gonna expect the fires to do. So, we were actually kept very well informed.

The community liaison then passed the information on to evacuees.

Community members who stay behind in evacuated communities – including members of the community leadership team, firefighters, or other residents – can be important sources of information. At Sandy Lake, the Chief produced daily video updates about the wildfire, its impacts on the community, and the safety of evacuees' houses and pets. The videos were uploaded onto the community's website and shared by evacuees using social media. Many evacuees recalled that their experience would have been much worse in the absence of this information:

It was a feeling of relief. And it was so good to know that our community was still here, because day by day we were always getting updates from our Chief over the internet. And we'd always check. And that was something we always would hover around, whoever brought a laptop or something, we'd all look at it. And he did it in our language – and he did it in English – for the Elders to understand too. And I was really proud of him for doing what he did and staying back.

As former evacuees reveal, social media is one of the most effective ways to ensure that community members hear about the status of the wildfire and its impacts from those remaining in the community, which can help to dispel rumours that often spiral out of control. A resident of Stanley Mission explained: "Everything was on Facebook. You gotta go on Facebook. That's the only way. You couldn't really talk to anybody because the phone lines for the Chief and council was pretty busy."

Other people who stay behind can also provide valuable information. Evacuees from Onion Lake recalled that the fire chief from Onion Lake Fire Rescue and Peacekeepers, who is also a local resident, provided helpful information. As previously mentioned, residents who stay behind in the community can also update evacuees on the status of their house and belongings. One woman explained that her son, who was fighting the fire, let her know that her house was okay. Another evacuee recalled that his uncle had let him know that nothing had burned down: "So everybody was really relieved of everything."

Information Sharing in Host Communities
Community liaisons and host communities can post or pass along information in evacuation centres or hotels. In the case of Taché, information was passed along during meals in Bushe River, over the band's radio station, and when band employees visited hotel rooms. During their 2014 evacuation, evacuees from Stanley Mission heard announcements made over the loudspeaker system at the Soccer Centre.

> Daily updates alleviate fears and stress and help evacuees ignore rumours.

These daily updates alleviate fears and stress and help evacuees ignore rumours. Evacuees worry about their houses, pets, and other possessions. Because of housing shortages on reserves, the loss of a house could mean homelessness for many families. Members of Whitefish Lake heard that houses had been lost, which turned out to be false. One resident recalled: "Because you don't know what's going on in the fire, you can't go back in there. And then there were

The Sandy Lake First Nation's Fire Department. A 2013 report by the office of the Auditor General of Canada found that funding for emergency-management programs on reserves is insufficient.
Photo: Henok Afsaw

people telling us that the whole community burnt ... Yeah, there were stories going around, all kinds of stuff. Most of this area was burnt, this area was burnt, your house is burnt, but we didn't know."

Evacuees also need to be provided with information about their family members, particularly if they have been sent to separate host communities, a major source of stress for many evacuees. Finding out this information requires a great deal of organization. During the evacuation of Sandy Lake, for example, evacuees were scattered throughout Ontario into nine different communities. One youth later recalled that he and his brothers could not communicate with their parents: "My brothers and I didn't know what to do. I kept asking who was in charge, and the people are, like, 'We don't know who's in charge.'"

In this case, to help evacuees locate family members, the Canadian Red Cross had set up a hotline. However, some evacuees never received information about the hotline and did not know who or where to call. Some contacted community leaders back in Sandy Lake for information, but the leaders had not received information from Emergency Management Ontario about where residents had been sent. One resident remembered:

> I think one of the things that really bugged me was each plane that left, nobody knew where they were going. I think that was one of our main challenges we had because every plane that we were sending out with parents, the mothers and their babies and some children, not every mother could take all their children with them, so they were split up. So the father would say, "Okay, where my wife going?" and we had no idea. We had no clue where they were going, so we couldn't tell them. So that's where we had quite a bit of challenge.

Because of difficulties using official information sources, evacuees turned to community websites, social media, and calling other community members to find family members. A group of youths created a closed Facebook group, "Sandy Lake First Nations Evac Info," to connect with family and other community members.

How to Share Knowledge with Evacuees

Organizers should keep in mind that traditional news media are not a reliable source of information for evacuees because they rarely report on all communities or give daily updates. At minimum, evacuees should be kept up to date on the wildfires through
- briefing sessions by community leaders
- daily announcements in host communities.

These announcements can be made in multiple ways:
- updates via band radio stations
- daily text or video updates on band websites
- postings on Facebook, Twitter, and other social media
- community liaisons or postings in hotels and evacuation centres

- announcements at meals
- hotlines to help locate family members
- closed information-sharing groups on Facebook.

Caring for Evacuees with Health Conditions and Day-to-Day Living

In addition to keeping evacuees informed, caring for evacuees with health conditions can pose extra challenges. Evacuation planners and organizers should be aware that First Nations communities have higher rates of many diseases than Canadians in general:

- Asthma is 40 percent more prevalent among First Nations, Inuit, and Métis communities than non-Indigenous communities.
- Indigenous Peoples are one and a half to two times more likely to develop heart disease than other Canadians.
- Indigenous People have a rate of diabetes three to five times higher than other Canadians.

Individuals with these conditions are usually evacuated first, and they typically have to stay away from the home community for longer, usually until health care services have been restarted. They also have special dietary needs and require more personal care.

One evacuee explained the difficulties she encountered during the evacuation of Whitefish Lake: "I can't walk very good. My leg was swelling up, and diabetes, 'cause my blood sugar was shooting up, I was feeling sick. That's all I remember most of the time when we were up there. The nurses would change my bandage." Evacuees from Taché likewise recalled the problems that asthma sufferers encountered in High Level when the wind switched direction, blowing smoke into the host community and forcing people to stay inside their motel rooms: "Yeah, we all stayed together in one room, but I had to keep my grandson [with asthma] in the room most of the time because of the smoke ... There was smoke all over the place, so we mostly stayed in the room and watched TV with him, occupied him." The fact that the hotel did not have air conditioning made the situation worse. The band provided bottled water, but evacuees recalled being hot and having difficulties breathing. A few had severe reactions to the smoke and spent time in hospital on Ventolin.

> To ensure that evacuees get the care they need, a designated community liaison should be stationed in each host community to provide information and support.

To ensure that evacuees get the care they need, designated community liaisons should be stationed in each host community to provide information and support. But making sure this happens can be a challenge. During the evacuation of Sandy Lake First Nation, for example, there were not enough community liaisons to serve the large number of designated host communities. The community liaison's responsibilities can also be wide-ranging and overwhelming. During the evacuation of Mishkeegogamang in 2011, for example, community liaisons attended daily information briefings, helped organize activities, arranged for medication for evacuees who forgot to bring theirs, provided transportation for evacuees, and organized security to keep evacuees safe. During the evacuation of Stanley Mission, community liaisons provided translation services (Cree to English and vice versa) and assisted with shopping, laundry, and child care. They also helped people from other communities who either didn't have community liaisons or were visiting the evacuation centres. In a similar vein, community liaisons from Mishkeegogamang explained that they helped the community liaison from Sandy Lake who was solely responsible for looking after 450 evacuees in Sioux Lookout.

Liaisons and organizers should also encourage evacuees to help one another. During the evacuation of Mishkeegogamang, for example, residents volunteered to help care for young children and Elders; they assisted with housekeeping, cooking, and cleaning the hotel; and they helped to arrange for benefit cheques for evacuees.

One volunteer recalled:

> When parents would have to go out and do laundry or something like that, I would try to provide child care. 'Cause some of the kids would get overwhelmed, and they'd be all over the place; some of them in a new environment ... especially with parents who had five, six kids with them, and they're all running around. So I tried to provide child care out there.

Providing child care is important, particularly for families with multiple or high-risk children. In the latter case, women and their children are often separated from the rest of their family during evacuations.

Other volunteer activities can include ensuring that evacuees in alternative accommodations have food, water, and necessities; providing security at hotels and evacuation centres; and serving as liaisons with other agencies. During the evacuation of Stanley Mission, for example, an evacuee who stayed in Prince Albert volunteered to be a liaison for the Red Cross. Another evacuee with experience living in the city helped alleviate culture shock by showing people how to take taxis and read street signs. Evacuees found that the experience brought community members closer together. However, volunteering during an evacuation can bring additional stress – not only is the volunteer supporting community members, he or she is also dealing with the stress of being an evacuee and supporting their own families.

Guiding Questions for First Nations

- How can you share information with evacuees during the evacuation to help reduce their stress? Who will share this information?
- Could videos be used to provide daily updates to evacuees?
- Can your website or social media be used to share information with evacuees?

- Does your emergency plan include a process for letting the host community know which community members have health conditions?
- In your evacuation plan, are there enough community liaisons identified in case the community is separated during an evacuation?
- Are there ways to provide support to community liaisons to help them carry out their role and lessen distress during an evacuation?

Guiding Questions for Host Communities

- Are there places where community members can share meals together?
- Is culturally appropriate food available for evacuees, particularly Elders?
- Can food be provided on a flexible schedule so that evacuees can minimize disruption to their usual meal schedule?
- Can snacks and other refreshments be available to evacuees when they are hungry and thirsty outside the designated meal times?
- Have activities been arranged for evacuees, including children, youth, adults, and Elders?
- How will local residents be encouraged to become involved or to volunteer to support evacuees and the host community?
- Are there local Indigenous organizations or nearby First Nations that can help arrange culturally appropriate food and activities?
- Are there activities that community members normally participate in at home that can be organized in a host community?
- If evacuees stay outside a designated host community, do they have activities to keep them busy during the evacuation?
- How will racist incidents be dealt with? Will there be a formal reporting mechanism?

Community Spotlight

Sandy Lake First Nation, Ontario

Sandy Lake First Nation is located seventy kilometres northeast of the Deer Lake First Nation reserve, along the banks of Neh gaaw saga'igan, or Sandy Lake. It is one of the largest First Nations in northern Ontario, with an estimated population of 3,000 as of May 2015, most of whom live on reserve. Sandy Lake is a fly-in community, but a winter road joins it with Deer Lake and North Spirit Lake First Nation for roughly six weeks in the winter. Sandy Lake also connects to Keewaywin First Nation by boat between April and November. Community members practise traditional activities such as fishing, hunting, trapping, and harvesting seasonally available wild animals and plants (mainly berries). Local animals and plants remain the major source of food, supplementing limited, lower-quality, and costly store-bought food.

In mid-July 2011, a series of lightning storms sparked forest fires across the boreal forests of northern Ontario, causing the evacuation of Sandy Lake. On July 18, the Chief announced a partial evacuation of approximately 950 residents at high risk from smoke, and two days later a full community evacuation was ordered. The evacuation lasted for ten days for most evac-uees and an additional week for those who were at risk from smoke.

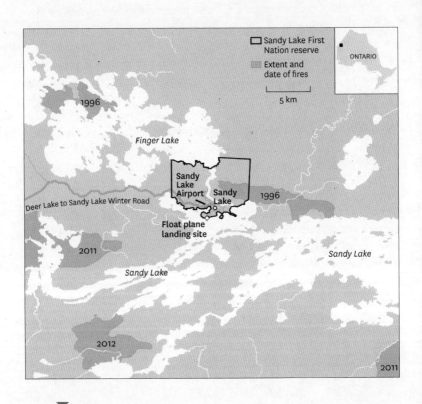

The fly-in community of Sandy Lake
First Nation was evacuated after
lightning strikes caused nearby
wildfires in 2011.

6.

RETURNING HOME

Maybe that's why I'm just terrified of forest fires now.
— COMMUNITY MEMBER, ONION LAKE FIRST NATION

It took the evacuation to make me realize the things I took for granted and that there was a lot to lose.
— COMMUNITY MEMBER, WHITEFISH LAKE FIRST NATION

EVACUEES EXPERIENCE NOTHING but relief when they hear the announcement that they can return home. Some have been away for weeks and have endured challenges such as loneliness, poor accommodations, and being separated from family. The immediate threat might be over, but community leaders and members of outside agencies should be aware that the evacuation's effects will linger in individual and communal memories for weeks, months, and even years. Community members will need assistance financially and emotionally. Some individuals will experience severe anxiety at the sight or smell of smoke. Some bands will struggle to deal with the financial repercussions. The stories and recollections of former evacuees point to key areas where community leaders and external agencies can concentrate their efforts to ensure the smoothest transitions through key stages of the process:

- lifting the evacuation order and informing the community
- celebrating the return home
- taking stock
- dealing with immediate fears and loss
- recognizing lasting impacts
- managing the financial repercussions.

Burned forest near Taché. The wildfire risk can be high during what is known as the "spring dip." *Photo: Kyla Mottershead*

As with the evacuation itself, responsibility for decision making differs from province to province and should be clarified in the evacuation plan.

Lifting the Evacuation Order and Informing the Community

Ultimately, the weather often decides: a shift in temperature from hot and dry to cool and wet can signal that the return home is imminent. In the Dene Tha' First Nation community of Taché, for example, the 2012 evacuation ended after seven days, on July 17, when air-monitoring machines set up by Health Canada indicated that these shifts had rendered it safe for residents to return home. Although the wildfire continued, it did not pose a direct threat to the community. Evacuees learned about the decision through a variety of channels, including

- notices posted in motels
- visits to motels from band employees
- word of mouth from family
- announcements during meals.

Factors That Can
Delay the Return Home

Although the decision to end the evacuation is often based
on the weather, sometimes other factors delay the return
home, which can be frustrating for evacuees who want to
return immediately after the threat has diminished. Time is
often needed to assess damage to the community (including
infrastructure and property damage) and to ensure that the
community is safe and that essential services are up and
running. For instance, during wildfire events power lines are
often burned and they can take weeks or months to rebuild.
Officials must then make sure generators and gas are available
to power community buildings, such as the health centre or
band office.

They heard that residents without vehicles could return by bus
and that each person would obtain a local grocery voucher valued
at forty dollars to replace food lost because of spoilage, which was
minimal because there had been no electricity blackouts. Residents
with their own vehicles were told they could obtain a forty-dollar
purchase order to replace gasoline used during the evacuation.

At Onion Lake Cree Nation, which experienced partial evacuations in 2012 and 2013, smaller fires meant that evacuees could
return home quickly once they were under control. Some evacuees
returned home in the evening; others stayed away overnight. The
fire chief or family members informed evacuees they could return,
but because dry conditions persisted, they remained on guard.

During the 2014 and 2015 evacuations of Stanley Mission, residents had to wait for approval from the Saskatchewan Ministry
of Health before they could return to the community, and some
people had to wait until essential services were up and running on
the reserve. Once the ministry tested air-quality levels and deemed
them acceptable, the Red Cross arranged for transportation home.
Evacuees heard the news through loudspeakers in the evacuation
centres. One resident recalled:

They announced it on the intercom. We packed up, and they said Stanley Mission and [another community] will be getting the first buses. So we went and waited, and they called us, I think, so we were rushing, and we got ready, and they called our names on to the buses and we got on. No, they took our names down while we were hoppin' on the bus; they were askin' for our names.

Evacuees were given fifteen dollars per person to buy food and drink for the long bus ride. Once they left the evacuation centre, organizers moved people with chronic health conditions to hotel rooms.

For fly-in communities, repatriation can be a complex process because aircraft have to be arranged through external agencies. During the 2011 evacuation of Sandy Lake First Nation, which lasted ten days, community members such as nurses returned first so that all essential services would be available and fully operational when everyone returned. The people who had evacuated on July 20 during the full community evacuation returned home on July 29. The residents who had left during the partial evacuation on July 18, however, were forced to remain in the host community for an additional week because of smoke from surrounding fires. Travel arrangements for repatriating residents were made by Ontario's Ministry of Natural Resources and Forestry and Emergency Management Ontario and then communicated to the Chief. The Chief then informed evacuees about the details of the return schedule through video updates. With the use of smaller commercial airplanes, the repatriation took eight days.

Celebrating the Return Home
The arrival home is particularly momentous for fly-in communities who experience long evacuations and come home to welcome parties at the airport followed by community feasts. In Sandy Lake, the Chief and others who had stayed behind greeted planes at the community airport with a big "Welcome Home" sign, and volunteers registered all returning evacuees. Those without vehicles either boarded buses for the drive home or got rides from community residents with cars.

As many recalled, returning home was cause for celebration:

> When we got home, after that it was plane after plane, and we were driving everybody home, and it was just exciting. And you can just see the excitement on the people's faces, and the children were so excited to be home. They were just hugging us. It's almost like a child who's never seen a lollipop, that type of look. And it was just truly amazing to see those children just come to you and give you a big hug getting off that plane.

Once they arrived home, the Chief, through the community radio, advised residents to throw out food in their refrigerators and freezers. Everyone also enjoyed a feast, held at the Traditional Site, to welcome community members home and feed residents who could not afford to buy groceries. At the ceremony, the Chief presented a plaque to the people who had stayed behind to protect the community, an important action that is often forgotten.

The atmosphere at Deer Lake First Nation was likewise celebratory. When the first partial evacuation order was lifted after a week on July 13, 2011, residents returned home from Geraldton by plane. The second partial evacuation, which began on July 21, lasted for two weeks. When the evacuees arrived home, a community feast was held to welcome them. One resident who had not evacuated recalled:

> Once we knew everybody got back home, we just did a big fish fry to welcome home. So we got all the guys to go out fishing. They like to cook, so we had all the guys cook for the wives and the children that came home. About a week after that, I did my walk again, everything went back to normal. You could hear the kids splashing in the water. Everything went back to normal. But when they were gone, didn't feel like home. Do you know what I mean?

Although these fly-in communities celebrated the end of the evacuation, many former evacuees from other First Nations recalled that their communities had had no celebration or community meetings at all and no recognition of community members who had worked or volunteered for the community during the evacuation.

Taking Stock

Evacuees will want to talk about what happened during a community debrief. Former evacuees reported that, without this discussion, they felt they had no closure. These discussions can be difficult to organize, however. Staff, community liaisons, and volunteers recalled being completely exhausted once they returned home, having worked as many as twenty hours a day for weeks. Many said they took their vacation time as soon as they arrived home to recover from the ordeal.

> Evacuees will want to talk about what happened during a community debrief. Without this discussion, they will feel like they have no closure.

Residents from communities that did have celebrations, however, said the feast provided a forum to offer and extend support to community members in need and to discuss what happened during the evacuation. In other communities, everyone was too busy, and the meetings never happened. Many former evacuees said that everyone just got on with their normal life. A few parents recalled that their children cried because they wanted to go back to the city, but youth seemed happy to return home to see friends. Youth from Whitefish Lake First Nation said they were happy to go back to school because they had a chance to talk with friends about the evacuation. By contrast, an adult from the same community said she spoke to no one about the evacuation.

Residents from Taché said they wanted a community meeting where they could discuss their experiences and provide feedback to leadership. These meetings can also open a space for the community to acknowledge the contributions of volunteers, as happened at Sandy Lake. Residents were frustrated that nothing had been done to improve upon emergency-management procedures: "And then we never got any report of how it went, how they moved people and all that. So how would I know? They need to have a report done after everything's done. So, this is how we moved people, this is what we did."

> A community gathering can open a space for the community to acknowledge the contributions of volunteers, who are often overlooked.

Some former evacuees recalled being frustrated to learn that some evacuees and families had been given financial or other support that other families hadn't been aware of, leading to charges of favouritism. At Stanley Mission, for example, those who had to take the bus heard later that evacuees with private vehicles had been given gas money. They felt all evacuees should have been given an equal amount of money to spend as they wished. Others expressed concerns that families related to community leaders had been given special treatment. However, one resident expressed pride in how the evacuation had been handled: "I have to give my Chief a high five. She did a damn good job. She didn't let the white society push her around, and she really put her foot down ... She shoved right back and made me really proud. And I had the opportunity to say thank you for a job well done."

Dealing with Immediate Fears and Loss

Although it's important for community leaders and organizers to celebrate and mark the return home in some way, they also need to recognize that, for many community members, returning home can mean that the hard work of recovery has just begun. It can be demoralizing. Many return to homes that have had no power for weeks. Already tired and exhausted, they now have a tremendous amount of work, particularly cleaning or throwing out refrigerators and freezers full of now rotten wild and store-bought meat. Many evacuees identified this loss as a major setback, particularly since replacing wild meat requires a lot of effort.

When Mishkeegogamang Ojibway Nation returned home, residents likewise discovered that their food had spoiled. They recalled that it was a particularly difficult loss since there was no compensation:

The only sad part is nobody got reimbursed ... I heard a lot of people had to start from scratch again. I had full things of stuff in there, like moose meat, liver, and chicken, everything you could think of. They were no good when you came back. That's the only sad part. Everybody experienced that ... They gotta start from scratch again. I guess everybody had to start up again. Packing up stuff here and there. We usually harvest everything, especially in the summertime, harvest the fish. We start in August and start harvesting things so we can have things all year round.

At Onion Lake, where evacuees from the partial evacuations returned home on the evening of the evacuation or the next day, residents remained extremely fearful of the fire. One recalled: "Well, after we came back, I was terrified still. They had said they were still working on the fire but it was safe enough for us to come home. But they had mentioned something about the little fires that are still there." Another community member corroborated her statement: "Little fires. The next day my auntie comes cruising up the hill here. We were just settled in, and she comes cruising, 'There's a fire just on the other side here.' And I thought, *Oh, no, I'm not leaving again* ... We didn't really sleep until it was all contained." One person mentioned that children continued to be concerned: "They were really scared. They kept looking out the window at night. They don't sleep. It came too close to the house." Afterwards, the children were too scared to do normal activities outside such as having a campfire. Another community member had to go to the hospital because of a severe asthma flare-up from smoke inhalation.

Residents of Onion Lake said that no one followed up with them after the evacuation but that they would have appreciated support or

Firebreaks like this one near Stanley Mission can slow or stop the spread of wildfires, and give firefighters a safe area from which to fight a fire. *Photo: Larry Fremont, Government of Saskatchewan*

advice on how to get rid of the smoke smell or how to clean up their yards. One Elder noted that she had no one to express her fears to and no support from the band:

> They told us that they could ignite any time. So that kind of just scared me 'cause I wasn't used to having that kind of fire so close by. I was scared. To tell you the truth, I didn't wanna go to sleep. I was scared that, What if it happens again? I didn't have anybody to call. I didn't have no support. That's the one thing I didn't get was no support on, from the band level. I think it took me almost a week, it seems like. I didn't wanna stay here. I actually wanted to go and go visit my auntie who lives in North Battleford. That's how I felt. I didn't feel safe here.

Recognizing Lasting Impacts

The sight of the brilliant blue sky is never appreciated more than after an evacuation ends. Laughter in the kitchen with the family is felt in a different way. Although the return to normal life is cherished, in reality experiencing an evacuation has lasting effects. A thunderstorm on a hot, dry summer day now carries a different weight. The smell or sight of smoke can cause immediate worry.

Even years later, people can retain vivid memories of evacuations, as becomes clear when they're asked to recount their stories. In Taché, most residents said that they had not shared their experiences with anyone outside their immediate family until they participated in the First Nations Wildfire Evacuation Partnership. For some, sharing their experiences was difficult. One resident stated: "To be honest, I don't feel good right now having to go back and over what I experienced. It's just like that happened a couple days ago." Others likewise had difficulties sharing their experiences, stating that they were still struggling with the stress they had experienced during the evacuation and the lack of resources available to help them cope: "I feel still stressed. I never dealt with any of it ... and there was no counsel or nothing put in place for people that would have been affected, and how it affected them, and how stressful it was ... I don't know how they run everything."

Other community members from Taché reported that certain sights and smells triggered their memories of the 2012 evacuation, causing them to worry about their ability to cope with a similar situation. One person recalled: "We saw helicopters the other day, and we're, like, 'Oh, no, we're gonna get evacuated again.' Everybody's like, 'Oh, no,' and we all start talking about it again."

At Whitefish Lake, a few residents said they were still dealing with the emotional toll and that their children also feared being evacuated again. Seeing smoke in the sky, a common summer occurrence, triggered these concerns. As one resident explained: "Kinda just scared, lookin' over to see if it will happen again. I don't really want it to happen again. If I see fires, I'm wanting to go put it out and control it or even watch it or whatnot. That's how scared I am of fires that start over here. I don't wanna lose anything over here." At Sandy Lake, a community liaison said that whenever she sees smoke, she makes sure she is mentally prepared to fulfill her role:

With this evacuation, I'm sure it's in the back of everybody's head. They haven't forgotten. It's just right there. Everybody has their own experiences, how they felt, and I'm sure it's still with them. It's been how many years? And I feel like I'm just going through it again, just talking about it. My friend ... we always say to each other whenever we see smoke, "Are you ready? Do you think you're ready to do it again?" And I am always, like, "Be prepared."

A member of Mishkeegogamang likewise expressed this fear: "I wasn't ready. I wasn't even ready to leave at all when I left. So next time, I'll remember to be prepared."

While some people raised concerns about their level of preparedness, there were mixed feelings among others about whether they'd leave if there was another evacuation. Three residents from Whitefish Lake revealed the range of opinions that can exist in the community:

- "If there was another evacuation I'd wait until I had no choice, [until] the fire was right here somewhere, and depending on the wind blowing where."
- "I don't think I would. I'd evacuate across the lake. At least there I don't feel small."
- "I would probably leave. No point in making a big deal of it. You leave for a couple of days, that's good on you. Vacation."

Those who remained in the community during past evacuations said they intended to stay behind in the event of a future wildfire. In the words of one: "They don't have a right to kick me out of my community. This is my home. I wanna choose to die in my house burning, that's my choice."

Keeping Track of Expenses

During an evacuation, it is vital that evacuated First Nations keep track of all expenses associated with the evacuation. Doing so will ensure that the band is reimbursed for as many expenses as possible; it will also help to reduce work down the road, when claims need to be filed. If possible, band administrative staff should be assigned to record keeping during the evacuation. They should keep track of

- the names, ages, and contact information of all evacuees (not just heads of households, although those individuals should be noted)
- the evacuation location for each evacuee (hotel name, evacuation centre, campground)
- the date of evacuation for each evacuee
- bills from local gas stations
- cash handed out during the evacuation to meet evacuees' immediate needs (including justification)
- staffing expenses associated with the evacuation
- loss of or damage to infrastructure (including descriptions and photos, if possible).

At Sandy Lake, one-quarter of former evacuees said they would prefer to stay behind because of their former experiences. One resident explained:

I think there is a feeling that "never again." People do not want to go ever again. It is not because they are treated badly out there; it is just because that is an awful thing to go through. I think people would be more reluctant next time. It was chaos; families were really struggling because families were torn apart. Daily life was turned upside down. But the important thing is people were safe. But people do not want to go through the evacuation again.

At Mishkeegogamang, four out of five former evacuees who either did not want to leave or had stayed behind during the last evacuation said they planned to remain in their home on reserve, in a cabin, or at a lake in Mishkeegogamang Traditional Territory. Several participants from Taché said they'd stay because they did not think the last evacuation had been warranted for all residents. One explained: "First of all, you tell me how far the fire is, 'cause I don't have any health problems ... If it's like 200 kilometres or whatever away, I'm gonna stay home."

As explained in Chapter 1, community leaders and evacuation planners should take these community members' feelings into account because they cannot be forced to leave, and their assessments of what went wrong are useful for future evacuations. In general, residents remember evacuations as one of the toughest experiences to go through, but some recognize that these experiences will make it easier to carry out another evacuation. As a member of Sandy Lake stated: "I don't wish to be evacuated, but I have full confidence in the community, the leadership, and if we have to do it all over again, then it'll be more organized than before."

Managing the Financial Repercussions

After an evacuation is over, expense reimbursement can be a complicated process, particularly because of jurisdictional issues. Disaster-recovery programs are often covered by the provincial government because emergency management is under provincial jurisdiction. However, because First Nations are under federal jurisdiction, the situation can differ from province to province, depending on whether they have an agreement with the federal government that expenses will be covered by provincial or federal programs. Community leaders responsible for evacuations should reach out to their local Indigenous Services Canada regional office before an emergency for clarification on the reimbursement process in their area.

Most First Nations pay the costs associated with evacuations upfront and then these expenses are reimbursed later. Depending on the province, bands will either submit financial information to the provincial emergency-management agency or to Indigenous Services Canada directly. The submission must include evidence for all expenses. For some expenses, the process is relatively straightforward but still onerous. For others, such as cash handed out to meet immediate needs, it is nearly impossible. First Nations must devote considerable staff to the process of cost recovery, which limits their ability to accomplish regular tasks, such as providing services to band members. Some First Nations and individuals experience significant delays in recovering the costs, and some are never reimbursed for the total costs.

At Whitefish Lake, for example, the band paid the costs associated with the evacuation and then applied to the provincial government for reimbursement. But the process proved to be confusing and time-consuming, and the band could not claim all expenses incurred. One resident recalled:

> Financially, I think when a disaster happens, keep everything together, because if you don't ... you're just gonna lose money, because that's what we did and we're still recovering ... We were in receivership ... [then the] fire, and it was a costly time.

During the evacuation, many large families required more than one hotel room, but the band was only reimbursed for one room per family. The band also paid some members for mileage but could not provide proof of these payments, so the costs were not reimbursed. Three years following the evacuation, in 2014, the band had only been reimbursed $500,000 of the $700,000 spent on the evacuation. Already in receivership when the evacuation occurred, the band had trouble paying for water- and sewage-treatment plants damaged because of a power outage during the wildfire, and it could not afford to fix ongoing maintenance problems with the water-treatment plant, which was due for replacement in 2017.

In Taché, organizers and band administrators worked countless hours over months to fill out paperwork and provide documentation for Alberta's disaster-recovery program. One participant explained that the difficulties with the process stemmed from frequent changes to the application process: "The process is really slow, and then every year they keep changing the way we have to do the paperwork, and then we have to make the changes." It took more than a year to be partially reimbursed; in the meantime, funds came out of the band's administrative budget.

On a positive note, after the large evacuations of 2011 and 2016, many external agencies realized the financial-reimbursement procedure was complicated and difficult. Significant changes have been made to ease the burden on First Nations after evacuations, but the process is still cumbersome.

Guiding Questions for First Nations

- How will you decide when to lift the evacuation order? Who will make that decision?
- How are you planning to repatriate members to your community when the evacuation ends? Are there transport options available?
- If the power supply to the community is interrupted during an evacuation, is there a plan for assisting residents with the removal of fridges or freezers and to ensure they have water? Will appliances be replaced at the expense of the band?
- Are you planning to hold a community meeting once evacuees return home, a meeting where everyone can talk about the evacuation and you can hear about band members' experiences?
- Are you planning to acknowledge specific community members for their contributions during the evacuation?
- What long-term supports are in place for evacuees upon returning home?
- Have you received clear instructions and outside assistance on the financial-reimbursement process?

Guiding Questions for External Agencies

- Do you have a transparent process for informing First Nations about the current wildfire risk, the repatriation process, and timelines?
- Do you have a plan to provide assistance to the First Nation as evacuees return home, both at the larger scale (e.g., power, infrastructure) and the personal scale (e.g., assisting evacuees with cleaning)?
- Will you provide long-term supports to the community to deal with the lasting impacts of the evacuation?
- Is your cost-recovery process for the First Nation clear? Do you provide assistance to bands as they go through the process to ensure they claim all eligible expenses?

Community Spotlight

Onion Lake Cree Nation, Saskatchewan

Located on the Alberta-Saskatchewan border, approximately fifty kilometres north of Lloydminster, Onion Lake Cree Nation sits on the southern extent of the boreal forest and is named after a nearby lake, where wild onion grows in abundance. The Nation consists of the Makaoo 120 reserve, which straddles the Alberta-Saskatchewan border, and the Seekaskootch 119 reserve, which is located in Saskatchewan. Together, the reserves cover 21,255 hectares. Onion Lake is a relatively large First Nation of 5,350 members, and approximately 3,200 members live on reserve. The community is surrounded by prairie and aspen parkland, and it has two highways that run through the reserves. The main wildfire risk to the community is from grass and deciduous stand fires, which are most likely to occur during the spring dip.

Onion Lake has four schools (including a Cree immersion school) and multiple band- and privately owned businesses. The majority of residents speak English, but half have knowledge of Cree, their traditional language. Onion Lake is unique in that it has its own policing and firefighting department, known as the Onion Lake Fire Rescue and Peacekeepers.

Onion Lake is in an area that frequently experiences wildfire, and a portion of the community was evacuated in 2012 and 2013. Unlike in other communities, the emergency-management response to the wildfires was handled internally with little assistance from outside government agencies. Provincial government assistance was only needed to provide accommodation for one family off reserve; other evacuees were relocated to an area of the reserve not affected by the wildfire.

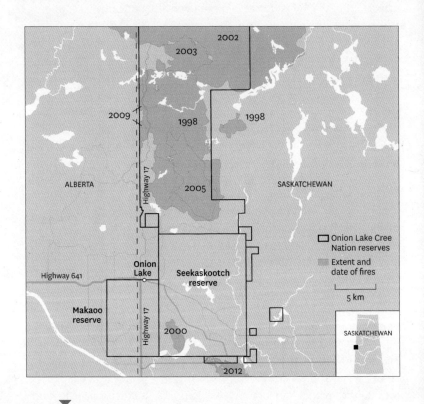

Onion Lake Cree Nation has
successfully undertaken wildfire
evacuations without assistance from
external agencies.

A Note on the Partnership

THE RESEARCH METHODS we used with each First Nation were similar, but there was some variation based on feedback from Chief and council, community advisers, and community research assistants.

The Research Team
Tara K. McGee is a non-Indigenous researcher with Irish heritage originally from Ottawa, Ontario. She completed her undergraduate degree at the University of Waterloo in environment and resource studies. After working in the social-impact assessment and public engagement field for a few years, she started her graduate studies. She completed her PhD at the Australian National University in Canberra, Australia, and then taught at Deakin University in Melbourne. While living in Melbourne, she completed a research project on wildfire preparedness in rural communities in Victoria, Australia. She returned to Canada in 2002 to take up a faculty position at the University of Alberta and has continued her research program in the human dimensions of wildfire ever since. Tara's research with Indigenous Peoples started with the supervision of Amy Christianson's PhD research with Peavine Métis settlement, which was followed by the First Nations Wildfire Evacuation Partnership. Her research has expanded to other projects, including research with Indigenous Peoples in the regional municipality of Wood Buffalo, which was affected by the 2016 Horse River (Fort McMurray) wildfire, and research with Māori in New Zealand.

    Amy Cardinal Christianson is Métis from northern Alberta, from the Laboucane-Cardinal families. After being forced west during European settlement of the Prairies, her great-grandparents settled in

Owl River, Alberta. They later moved to Fort McMurray so they could be closer to their children in mission school. Her extended family are fluent Cree-speakers who follow both Cree and Métis traditions and ceremonies. Amy grew up in the community of Whitecourt, Alberta, and she frequently experienced wildfires and smoke growing up. In 1997, the large Virginia Hills Fire resulted in heavy smoke in Whitecourt and fear among residents that the wildfire would enter the community. Amy completed her PhD research with Peavine Métis Settlement, which has become her second home. Amy currently lives in Rocky Mountain House, Alberta, and is an active member of the Métis Nation and an advocate for Indigenous wildfire stewardship. She currently works as a wildfire research scientist for the Canadian Forest Service (National Resources Canada), where she works with Indigenous Nations, organizations, and fire keepers from across Canada.

Henok Workeye Asfaw is a researcher from Ethiopia. Henok has a bachelor's degree in geography and a master's degree in development studies (specializing in environment and development) from Addis Ababa University in Ethiopia. As part of his master's degree, he spent several months with forest-dwelling Indigenous communities in southwest Ethiopia studying forest-based livelihoods and resource-management challenges. After completing his master's degree, Henok spent the next five years teaching and engaging in research at two public universities in Ethiopia. He taught undergraduate courses on the social-science aspects of disaster risk and environmental management, and he engaged in community-based studies in remote rural communities. He came to Canada in 2013 to undertake doctoral research at the University of Alberta, where he joined the First Nations Wildfire Evacuation Partnership. He was motivated to join the project and pursue his PhD because the project fell within his general research interest of disaster and emergency management, and it employed a community-based approach with remote Indigenous communities. Henok recently completed post-doctoral research with the Canadian Forest Service on community wildfire-mitigation preferences, and has now returned to manage the second phase of the First Nations Wildfire Evacuation Partnership.

The First Nations Wildfire Evacuation Partnership research team. *Left to right:* Henok Asfaw, Amy Christianson, Kyla Mottershead, and Tara McGee. *Photo: Tara McGee*

Kyla Mottershead is a non-Indigenous researcher, although her maternal side of the family has some distant First Nation heritage. Kyla grew up in northern British Columbia and moved to Alberta. In 2010, Kyla completed her undergraduate degree in development studies at the University of Calgary. She focused heavily on Indigenous studies, which brought her to the Peruvian Amazon, where she assisted with community-based research regarding the conservation and development issues of local Indigenous communities. Following her undergraduate degree, Kyla briefly returned to British Columbia to work for Pearson College before returning to Alberta to join the First Nations Wildfire Evacuation Partnership in 2013. Kyla completed her master's degree in 2017 and recently moved to New Zealand, where she now works for Te Pou o te Whakaaro Nui, an organization that supports workforce development for the mental health, addiction, and disability sectors. Kyla was interested in joining the partnership because of her interest in community-based research approaches and after

125

working with an Indigenous community to bring forth their experiences to help improve emergency management.

Karen Pheasant-Neganigwane is an Anishinaabe researcher from Wiikwemkoong on Manitoulin Island in Ontario. She is also a dancer, scholar, writer, artist, and orator. Her grandparents, maternal and paternal, come from Wiikwemkoong and her parents are residential school survivors. Karen was involved in the partnership from 2015 to 2017 as a research assistant, when she conducted interviews with evacuees from Onion Lake, Stanley Mission, and Deer Lake. At the time, she was enrolled in graduate studies in Educational Policy Studies/Indigenous Peoples Education at the University of Alberta. Her doctoral work incorporates the concept of Shiibaashka'igan (Jingle Dress), which represents the principle of healing. She is now an assistant professor at Mount Royal University in the Treaty Seven region.

Research Approach and Data Collection

The research for the First Nations Wildfire Evacuation Partnership was completed using qualitative methods, which have been found to be appropriate for studies with Indigenous communities.[1] We employed these methods to gain a better understanding of people's wildfire evacuation experiences and to bring to light unanticipated findings. We used a community-based approach that involved First Nations throughout the research process. Completing the research with seven First Nations enabled us to compare and contrast wildfire evacuation experiences and how evacuations were carried out;

---

1 See, for example, J. Kingsley, R. Phillips, M. Townsend, and C. Henderson-Wilson, "Using a Qualitative Approach to Research to Build Trust between a Non-Aboriginal Researcher and Aboriginal Participants (Australia)," *Qualitative Research Journal* 10, 1 (2010): 2–12; M.A. Maar, N.E. Lightfoot, M.E. Sutherland, et al., "Thinking Outside the Box: Aboriginal People's Suggestions for Conducting Health Studies with Aboriginal Communities," *Public Health* 125 (2011): 747–53; and S. Shahid, D. Bessarab, P. Howat, and S.C. Thompson, "Exploration of the Beliefs and Experiences of Aboriginal People with Cancer in Western Australia: A Methodology to Acknowledge Cultural Difference and Build Understanding," *BMC Medical Research Methodology* 9, 60 (2009): https://doi. org/10.1186/1471-2288-9-60.

The plane used to transport members of the First Nations Wildfire Partnership between Deer Lake and Sandy Lake during initial community visits. *Photo: Tara McGee*

it helped us to identify (1) factors that affected wildfire evacuation experiences and (2) ways to reduce the negative impacts of wildfire evacuations on First Nations.

Our research was influenced by the following books by Indigenous authors: Linda Tuhiwai Smith's *Decolonizing Methodologies*, Shawn Wilson's *Research Is Ceremony*, and Margaret Kovach's *Indigenous Methodologies*.[1] We would recommend these books to any researchers who want to work with Indigenous communities (particularly non-Indigenous researchers). This research was reviewed and approved by the University of Alberta's Research Ethics Committee, which concluded that it was consistent with the Tri-Council Policy Statement: Ethical Conduct for Research Involving Humans.[2] Ethics

---

1   Linda Tuhiwai Smith, *Decolonizing Methodologies: Research and Indigenous Peoples* (Dunedin, NZ: University of Otago Press, 1999); Shawn Wilson, *Research Is Ceremony* (Halifax, NS: Fernwood Publishing, 2009); and Margaret Kovach, *Indigenous Methodologies: Characteristics, Conversations, and Contexts* (Toronto: University of Toronto Press, 2010).

2   Canadian Institutes of Health Research, Natural Sciences and Engineering Research Council of Canada, and Social Sciences and Humanities Research Council of Canada, "Tri-Council Policy Statement: Ethical Conduct for Research Involving Humans," 2014, https://ethics.gc.ca/eng/policy-politique_tcps2-eptc2_initiatives.html.

clearance was renewed annually. Prior to starting this research, we also consulted with the First Nation Information Governance Centre.

The fieldwork was completed by members of the research team: Kyla Mottershead, Dene Tha' First Nation, Taché community; Tara McGee and Amy Christianson, Whitefish Lake First Nation 459; Karen Pheasant-Neganigwane, Onion Lake First Nation, Lac La Ronge Indian Band (Stanley Mission), and Deer Lake First Nation; Henok Asfaw, Sandy Lake First Nation; and Tara McGee, Mishkeegogamang Ojibway Nation. Community advisers, community research assistants, interview participants, and other community members also provided invaluable advice during the fieldwork.

The interviews completed within each First Nation were guided by a list of topics. Youths, adults, and Elders shared their evacuation experiences with us. We asked residents about

- their general experiences during the wildfire
- when and how they first heard about (or saw) the fire
- the evacuation process
- leaving the community
- their time away from the community
- returning home after the evacuation
- any lasting effects of the evacuation.

We also asked those who stayed behind about their experiences. The interviews were completed in a conversational style so that participants could tell their evacuation story in their own words. We then followed up to obtain further details about their experiences.

Deer Lake First Nation, Ontario

To start research with Deer Lake First Nation, Tara visited the community in September 2012 and spoke to the community leadership about the research, the partnership, and whether the Nation wanted to be involved. Henok then visited Deer Lake in July 2014 to undertake a preliminary study and learn about the 2011 wildfire evacuation. He met with key community leaders, health workers, and others who had a management role during the evacuation. A meeting was also held with Chief and councillors to explain the purpose of the planned research, the proposed research design, the data-collection procedures, and the desire to incorporate community input and feedback into the research design. In October 2016, Karen came on board and completed the fieldwork. Interview participants were selected through direct contact by the researcher and through referrals made by the participants and other key contacts. Karen conducted twenty-two semi-structured interviews with evacuated residents, those who stayed behind, and people who had a management role during the evacuation.

Dene Tha' (/'dɛnɛ ðɑ:) First Nation, Taché, Alberta

We contacted the Dene Tha' community of Taché in 2013 to see if they were interested in participating in the partnership. In the fall, Tara, Amy, and Kyla met with the First Nation's director of emergency management to get a better understanding of the evacuation and how it had occurred. They then met with the Chief and council in February 2014 to discuss the planned research, confirm their interest in participating, establish a community advisory committee, and begin the recruitment of two community research assistants. Kyla travelled to Taché in June 2014 to complete the first set of interviews and in August 2014 to complete the second. During the second trip two community research assistants, Tina Yakinneah and Cameron Chalifoux, helped her recruit interview participants and conduct interviews, and they translated from Dene Dhah to English when required and provided advice about the initial data analysis. Kyla returned to Dene Tha' First Nation and Taché in April 2015 to present and confirm the initial findings, and she presented the final report in May 2017.

In total, twenty-seven interviews were conducted with thirty-one participants. Participants included ten men and twenty-one women ranging in age from twenty to seventy-three years. They included people who evacuated, people who stayed home, and people involved in organizing the evacuation. Participants were recruited by the research assistants or via referrals from other interview participants and key contacts. Recruitment continued until no new information emerged from the interviews.

Lac La Ronge Indian Band, Stanley Mission (Amuchewaspimewin), Saskatchewan

While we were selecting community partners, our agency partners in Saskatchewan also suggested approaching Lac La Ronge Indian Band to learn more about the experiences of evacuees during the evacuation of Stanley Mission in May 2014. The Chief and council were approached and agreed to partner with us. Amy followed up with the councillors from Stanley Mission and received permission to interview residents. Karen undertook the data collection over the summer of 2015. While she was completing the interviews, a second evacuation of vulnerable residents took place because of wildfire smoke. We were therefore able to learn about wildfire evacuation experiences in both 2014 and 2015. In total, sixteen interviews were completed with twenty women and eleven men. Participants were recruited by the research assistant and via referrals from other interview participants and key contacts. In May 2017, Amy visited the community to discuss the initial results.

Mishkeegogamang Ojibway Nation, Ontario

Research with Mishkeegogamang Ojibway Nation started with a phone conversation between Tara and Chief Connie Gray-McKay, which was then followed by a visit to Mishkeegogamang in September 2013 to meet in person with the Chief and councillors to discuss the research, seek advice about the research process, and start to learn about Mishkeegogamang and the wildfire evacuation. Fieldwork was subsequently completed during three weeks in April 2014. Although a community research assistant was identified by the Chief, the person was unavailable to assist, so Tara completed the fieldwork with advice from the Chief and a community adviser. Research participants also helped by recruiting other interview participants and, in one case, by acting as an interpreter for an interview with an Elder.

Purposive sampling was used to recruit twenty-eight participants who had a variety of experiences, including four who had
formal roles during the evacuation, twelve who had evacuated to
the three host communities, four who stayed in other communities,
and five residents who stayed behind or near the reserve. In addition, interviews were completed with three participants who worked
in Mishkeegogamang but lived in Pickle Lake and were not evacuated. Interview participants included people in different age groups
(including three youths and three Elders), people who were single
and people with family responsibilities, and four parents who had
young children at the time of the evacuation. Unfortunately, a community tragedy prevented Tara from returning to Mishkeegogamang
to present initial findings and receive feedback, so the initial results
were instead sent to Chief Connie Gray-McKay for her review and
comments. At the end of the research, Tara tried to present findings
in Mishkeegogamang but due to a storm she was unable to fly to
the community. Instead, Tara met with former Chief Gray-McKay to
discuss the research findings.

Onion Lake (wîhcekaskosîwi-sâkahikanihk) Cree Nation, Saskatchewan

While we were selecting community partners, our agency partners
in Saskatchewan suggested approaching Onion Lake Cree Nation
because of their successful internal handling of a wildfire evacuation event in 2012. We approached Onion Lake Fire Rescue and
Peacekeepers, and they agreed to partner with us for the research.
In May 2013, Tara and Amy were invited to the Nation to observe
the emergency management of the Montanaville Fire and flood.
We spent the day with the emergency-management team and were
given a community tour. During this time, we met briefly with the
current Chief Wallace Fox to speak with him about the research
process. In fall 2013, Amy participated in a debrief meeting about
the flood response with outside agencies, including a discussion of
a report written about the event. All agencies praised Onion Lake's
response; however, everyone agreed that communication between

departments in the community and between the community and outside agencies could be improved.

In May 2014, Amy spoke by phone with the Chief and council to obtain their approval to interview residents about their evacuation experiences. Two research assistants were then hired: Adrian Waskewitch (from Onion Lake Cree Nation) and Karen Pheasant-Neganigwane (from Wiikwemkoong First Nation). They conducted interviews over the summer of 2015 with evacuees from the 2012 and 2013 wildfires. In total, eight interviews were completed with nine women and three men. Participants were recruited by the research assistants and via referrals from other interview participants and key contacts. Amy presented the initial results to the Chief and council at a National Treaties 1–11 Gathering in Edmonton, Alberta.

Sandy Lake First Nation (Neh gaaw saga'igan), Ontario

Tara first visited the Sandy Lake First Nation in September 2012 to speak to community leaders about the research and to confirm their interest in joining the partnership. In July 2014, Henok visited the community to learn about the 2011 wildfire evacuation; he met with key community leaders, health workers, and others who had a management role during the evacuation. A community research advisory committee consisting of three members was established to provide guidance. On the recommendation of committee members, research assistant Charles Anishinabie, who was knowledgeable about the community and spoke Oji-Cree, was recruited. During this initial visit, six key contact interviews were conducted with people involved in carrying out the evacuation, including community leaders, people who had stayed behind to provide support, health workers, and people who were assigned as community liaison officers at the host communities. The knowledge gained during this visit helped shape the study proposal and design questions included in the interview guide.

During a second visit in July and August 2015, fifty-six interviews were completed – forty with evacuated residents and sixteen with residents who had stayed behind, including community leaders, health workers, front-line workers, and other residents who helped with the evacuation. Two focus groups were conducted: the first with councillors and Elders, the second with a youth group. A combination of purposive, snowball, and convenience sampling techniques were employed to recruit interview participants. The process ended at the point of saturation – when interviews yielded no new information.[1] Following initial data analysis, Henok went back to Sandy Lake to share the research results via booklets and a presentation to the band administration. After the presentation, the community provided feedback to improve future evacuations.

Whitefish Lake First Nation 459 (Atikameg), Alberta

To start the research with Whitefish Lake First Nation 459, Amy and Tara first met with the emergency-management officer and then visited the reserve to meet with councillors to find out if the community would be interested in being involved. Once the councillors gave their support, they identified two community advisers and two community research assistants to join our research team. During this visit, we also met with other band council staff to learn about the evacuation and the First Nation.

We undertook fieldwork during two visits to Whitefish in July and September 2014. Two trained community research assistants, Sharon Sahlin and Sheila Laboucan, provided us with advice, helped to recruit interview participants and conduct interviews, and acted as interpreters when required. Using purposive sampling to obtain a variety of perspectives, we completed thirty-one semi-structured interviews with forty-five band members, including thirty women and fifteen men in different age groups (seven Elders, ten youths, and twenty-eight other adults). We interviewed residents who were evacuated to host communities, residents who stayed elsewhere with family and friends, and residents who did not evacuate. Although most interviews were with individuals, five interviews were completed with two residents who wished to be interviewed together,

---

1   J.W. Creswell, *Qualitative Inquiry and Research Design: Choosing among Five Approaches*, 2nd ed. (Thousand Oaks, CA: Sage Publications, 2007).

Whitefish Lake research assistants Sharon Sahlin *(left)* and Sheila Laboucan *(right)* stop for a photograph with authors Tara McGee and Amy Cardinal Christianson *(middle)*.
Photo: Amy Cardinal Christianson

and we also met with four groups of youths. As part of the data analysis process, Amy returned to Whitefish Lake in March 2015 to discuss the initial results with the community advisers and to obtain feedback from councillors and other community contacts. Tara returned to Whitefish Lake at the beginning of May 2016 to present the community with the booklets and the poster we had produced.

Data Analysis

In each of the First Nations, the interviews were recorded, transcribed professionally, and checked for accuracy. We then analyzed the data qualitatively using thematic analysis and NVivo 10/11 software. We used a mix of descriptive and analytical coding to analyze the data. We used descriptive codes to label subjects such as accommodation, transportation, or other aspects of the evacuation. Descriptive codes also came from our review of the relevant academic literature and in early data analysis. Analytical codes were also used to label themes that arose from the data, including different experiences that arose during each stage of the evacuation process.

Researcher Henok Asfaw presents results to council members at Sandy Lake First Nation. *Photo: Henok Asfaw*

Dissemination of Research Findings

The main difficulty with this type of research is keeping all partners informed and involved from the beginning to the end of a research project. As always, interest wanes as the project progresses but picks up at the end when results are analyzed and discussed. Outside of the standard academic processes, we used various strategies to seek advice from and inform our partners, including teleconference calls, newsletters, a project website, group emails, personal emails, personal phone calls, in-person visits, and joint presentations. We disseminated the results in a number of ways. We held eight teleconference meetings with our partners, during which we sought their input, discussed issues, presented findings, and discussed recommendations. We prepared five newsletters. We gave presentations to the leaders of the seven First Nations and prepared community booklets for First Nations whose evacuation stories were told from the perspectives of interview participants. We also prepared short two-page summaries focusing on key findings and recommendations, which we then disseminated to our partners and posted on our website.

As a team, we gave thirty-two presentations about our research to local, regional, national, and international audiences. We gave fourteen media interviews, mainly during the 2016, 2017, and 2018 wildfire seasons in Alberta and British Columbia. During wildfire events in 2016, 2017, and 2018, we also gave advice on improving evacuations and urged federal and provincial government agencies to support those who choose to stay behind.

Working with a graphic designer, we prepared an infographic to present recommendations to emergency managers. We circulated the infographic on social media, including Facebook, LinkedIn, and Twitter. We had eleven thousand views on Twitter alone. Many agencies reached out to the research team to ask for permission to use the infographic in presentations or share it with staff. The International Association of Emergency Managers shared the infographic with its members.

Our website (https://sites.google.com/ualberta.ca/awe/home) describes the partnership and includes the infographic, the two-page summaries, other reports and documents, and a page of resources for First Nations. The website also includes a link to Kyla Mottershead's video about the First Nations Wildfire Evacuation Partnership, which was awarded an Honourable Mention in the Social Science and Humanities Research Council's 2015 Storytellers competition. Graduate students Henok Asfaw and Kyla Mottershead presented their research findings in their theses.[1] In addition to this guide, we have disseminated the results of our research findings in academic and practitioner journals. These publications are listed in the "Further Resources and References" section.

---

1 H.W. Asfaw, "Wildfire Evacuation and Emergency Management in Remote First Nations: The Case of Sandy Lake First Nation, Northern Ontario" (PhD diss., University of Alberta, 2018); and K.D. Mottershead, "The 2012 Wildfire Evacuation Experiences of Dene Tha' First Nation" (master's thesis, University of Alberta, 2017).

Acknowledgments

WE HAVE MANY people and organizations to thank for assisting us with the research carried out as part of the First Nations Wildfire Evacuation Partnership, which is presented in this book.

Our sincere thanks to the more than two hundred First Nation residents who participated in this research. We know that speaking to us caused some residents to relive their stressful evacuation experiences. Several residents told us that telling us their story, in some cases for the first time, was helpful. We hope that others also benefited from telling their evacuation stories. Thank you again for sharing your stories with us.

We also thank the community advisers and community research assistants who helped us by providing advice and support, suggesting and helping to recruit interview participants, assisting with interviews, and, in some cases, helping with translation. Thank you to Cameron Chalifoux and Tina Yakinneah (Dene Tha' First Nation), Charles Anishinabie (Sandy Lake First Nation), Adrian Waskewitch (Onion Lake First Nation), and Sheila Laboucan and Sharon Sahlin (Whitefish Lake First Nation). We also thank the many community members who provided us with assistance, advice, accommodation, and other support.

Thank you to the Chiefs and other community leaders of the seven First Nations who kindly permitted us to complete this research. In some cases, there was a change in First Nation leadership during the research, and we thank the new leaders for their continued support. Thank you to Deer Lake First Nation Chief Roy Dale Meekis and Howard Meekis; Dene Tha' Chief James Ahnassay, Linda Semansha, and Sidney Chambaud; Lac La Ronge Indian Band Chief Tammy Cook-Searson, Linda Charles, Larry Charles, Gordon Hardlotte, and Percy

Mirasty; Mishkeegogamang Ojibway Nation former Chief Connie Gray-McKay and Chief David Masakayash; Sandy Lake First Nation former Chiefs Bart Meekis and Adam Fiddler, councillor Fabian Crow, and Kenny Goodwin; and Whitefish Lake First Nation councillor Darren Auger, former Chief Robert Grey, and Paul Thunder.

Thank you to the agencies and other partners involved in the First Nations Wildfire Evacuation Partnership. Special thanks to Larry Fremont for drawing our attention to problems experienced by Indigenous Peoples during wildfire evacuations in Saskatchewan, which led to the development of this partnership. The organizations included in this partnership include the Alberta Emergency Management Agency, the Assembly of First Nations, the First Nations Emergency Service Society of BC, the Health Canada First Nations and Inuit Health Branch, the Ontario Ministry of Natural Resources and Forestry, the Saskatchewan Ministry of Environment's Wildfire Management Branch, the Saskatchewan Ministry of Government Relations, Indigenous and Northern Affairs Canada, the Saskatchewan Ministry of Government Relations – Public Safety, and the Saskatchewan Ministry of Health. We hope that the results of this research help guide future wildfire and emergency response policy and decision making within your agencies.

This research (and this book) would not have been possible without funding from the Social Sciences and Humanities Research Council of Canada. Our partnership-development grant enabled us to complete this research and bring together researchers, First Nations, and agencies in an attempt to reduce the impacts of wildfire evacuations on First Nations in Canada. The Alberta Centre for Child, Family, and Community Research (now PolicyWise for Children and Families), the Canadian Circumpolar Institute, and the University of Alberta (through a Northern Research Award) also provided funding for this research. Kyla Mottershead, MA, who completed research with Dene Tha' First Nation, received additional grants and scholarship support, including the Alberta Graduate Student Scholarship, the Canadian Circumpolar Institute CBAR Grant, the Eugene Brody Graduate Scholarship, the Northern Scientific Training Program

Grant, a Queen Elizabeth II Graduate Scholarship, and the Walter H. Johns Graduate Scholarship. Henok Asfaw, PhD, who completed the research with Sandy Lake First Nation, received the University of Alberta Northern Research Award in 2015–16 and 2016–17.

We would like to thank Karen Erickson for creating her beautiful piece, *Sunfire*, for the partnership and for allowing us to share it in – and on – this book. As well, we would like to thank Jimmy Grey for generously providing us with his photos – including the one on the cover – of the Whitefish Lake First Nation wildfire in 2011. Sid Chambaud, Larry Fremont, Chico Halkett, Isabelle Hardlotte, Vicki Hardlotte, Marc Perreault, and Lynn Roberts also contributed photos; we are grateful to them as well.

We were very fortunate to work with such a wonderfully supportive team at UBC Press. Thank you to Darcy Cullen who enthusiastically supported our book proposal. Nadine Pedersen had the vision of turning our academic work into this practical guide, and encouraged and supported us through this transition and on through to the publication stage. Ann Macklem and colleagues at the press provided valuable guidance, assistance, and nudges. Many thanks Darcy, Nadine, and Ann. Our sincere thanks as well to substantive editor Lesley Erickson, who helped transform the results of our social science research into this guide.

The authors would especially like to raise up their families and friends for their support during the research process and writing of this book.

Further Resources and References

Online Resources

Alberta Health Services. "Wildfire Smoke and Your Health." https://myhealth.alberta.ca/Alberta/Pages/wildfire-smoke-health.aspx.

Government of Alberta. "Community Evacuation Guidelines and Planning Considerations." http://www.aema.alberta.ca/documents/community-evacuation-guidelines-planning-considerations-may-2018.pdf.

Indigenous Services Canada. "Emergency Management Assistance Program." https://www.sac-isc.gc.ca/eng/1534954090122/1535120506707.

–. "Fire Protection in First Nation Communities." https://www.sac-isc.gc.ca/eng/1317842518699/1535120096924.

–. "Indigenous Health." https://www.sac-isc.gc.ca/eng/1569861171996/1569861324236.

–. "Roles and Responsibilities during Emergencies." https://www.sac-isc.gc.ca/eng/1309372584767/1535120244606.

Ontario Ministry of the Solicitor General. "Ontario Mass Evacuation Plan Part 1: Far North." https://www.emergencymanagementontario.ca/english/emcommunity/response_resources/plans/mass_evacuation_plan.html.

Tŝilhqot'in National Government. "Nagwediẑk'an gwaneŝ gangu ch'inidẑed ganexwilagh (The Fires Awakened Us): Tsilhqot'in Report – 2017 Wildfires." http://www.tsilhqotin.ca/Portals/0/PDFs/2019_TheFiresAwakenedUs.pdf.

References

Asfaw, Henok W., Tara K. McGee, and Amy Cardinal Christianson. "Indigenous Elders' Experiences, Vulnerabilities and Coping during Hazard Evacuation: The Case of the 2011 Sandy Lake First Nation Wildfire Evacuation." *Society and Natural Resources,* 2020. https://doi.org/10.1080/08941920.2020.1745976.

–. "The Role of Social Support and Place Attachment during Hazard Evacuation: The Case of Sandy Lake First Nation, Canada." *Environmental Hazards* 18, 4 (2019): 361–81. https://doi.org/10.10 80/17477891.2019.1608147.

Asfaw, Henok W., Sandy Lake First Nation, Tara K. McGee, and Amy Cardinal Christianson. "Evacuation Preparedness and the Challenges of Emergency Evacuation in Indigenous Communities in Canada: The Case of Sandy Lake First Nation, Northern Ontario." *International Journal of Disaster Risk Reduction* 34 (March 2018): 55–63. https://doi.org/10.1016/j.ijdrr.2018.11.005.

–. "A Qualitative Study Exploring Barriers and Facilitators of Effective Service Delivery for Indigenous Wildfire Hazard Evacuees during Their Stay in Host Communities." *International Journal of Disaster Risk Reduction* 41 (December 2019). https:// doi.org/10.1016/j.ijdrr.2019.101300.

Bensadoun, Emerald. "Pikangikum First Nation Evacuation Plan Paused Due to Lack of Host Communities: Chief." Canadian Press, July 10, 2019. https://globalnews.ca/news/5479131/ pikangikum-evacuation-paused-lack-host-communities/.

Christianson, Amy Cardinal, and Tara K. McGee. "Wildfire Evacuation Experiences of Band Members of Whitefish Lake First Nation 459, Alberta, Canada." *Natural Hazards* 98 (2019): 9–20. https://doi.org/10.1007/s11069-018-3556-9.

Fiddler, Willow. "Evacuation of Pikangikum to Continue Friday Ahead of Forest Fire." APTN News, May 30, 2019. https://www. aptnnews.ca/national-news/evacuation-of-pikangikum-to -continue-friday-ahead-of-forest-fire/.

Freeze, Colin, and Jeff Gray. "Residents Wait to Leave Pikangikum First Nation, a Week after Forest Fire Evacuation Order." *Globe and Mail*, July 12, 2019. https://www.theglobeandmail.com/canada/article-about-2000-residents-wait-to-leave-northern-ontario-town-a-week/.

Malone, Kelly Geraldine. "'It Got Worse': Evacuation Criticized after First Nation Surrounded by Fire." Canadian Press, May 23, 2018. https://www.680news.com/2018/05/23/manitoba-first-nation-community-trapped-by-smoke-as-fire-creeps-closer/.

McGee, Tara K. "Evacuating First Nations during Wildfires in Canada." *Fire Safety Journal*, May 4, 2020. https://doi.org/10.1016/j.firesaf.2020.103120.

McGee, Tara K., Amy Christianson, Henok W. Asfaw, and Kyla Mottershead. "Advice for Emergency Managers from the First Nations Wildfire Evacuation Partnership." HAZNET, May 2018.

McGee, Tara K., Mishkeegogamang Ojibway Nation, and Amy Christianson. "Residents' Wildfire Evacuation Actions in Mishkeegogamang Ojibway Nation, Ontario, Canada." *International Journal of Disaster Risk Reduction* 33 (February 2019): 266–74. https://doi.org/10.1016/j.ijdrr.2018.10.012.

Mottershead, Kyla, Tara K. McGee, and Amy Christianson. "Evacuating a First Nation Due to Wildfire Smoke: The Case of Dene Tha' First Nation." *International Journal of Disaster Risk Science* 11 (2020): 274–86. https://doi.org/10.1007/s13753-020-00281-y.

NEWS1130. "Forest Fire Prompts Full Evacuation of Pikangikum First Nation in Ontario." Canadian Press, July 8, 2019. https://www.citynews1130.com/2019/07/08/forest-fire-prompts-full-evacuation-of-pikangikum-first-nation-in-ontario/.

Office of the Auditor General of Canada. "Emergency Management on Reserves." Chapter 6, *2013 Fall Report of the Auditor General of Canada*. https://www.oag-bvg.gc.ca/internet/English/parl_oag_201311_06_e_38800.html.

Yumagulova, Lilia, Suzanne Phibbs, Christine Kenney, Darlene Yellow Old Woman-Munro, Amy Cardinal Christianson, Tara K. McGee, and Rosalita Whitehair. "The Role of Disaster Volunteering in Indigenous Communities." *Environmental Hazards,* August 29, 2019. https://doi.org/10.1080/17477891.2019.1657791.

Index